MW00582151

NOODLE WORSHIP

Easy Recipes for All the Dishes You Crave
from Asian, Italian and American Cuisines

LARONE &
TIFFANI THOMPSON

Creators of @NoodleWorship

PAGE STREET
PUBLISHING CO.

PAGE STREET
PUBLISHING CO.

Copyright © 2022 by Larone and Tiffani Thompson

First published in 2022 by
Page Street Publishing Co.
27 Congress Street, Suite 1511
Salem, MA 01970
www.pagestreetpublishing.com

All rights reserved. No part of this book may be reproduced or used, in any form or by any means, electronic or mechanical, without prior permission in writing from the publisher.

Distributed by Macmillan, sales in Canada by The Canadian Manda Group.

26   25   24   23   22   1   2   3   4   5

ISBN-13: 978-1-64567-528-0
ISBN-10: 1-64567-528-9

Library of Congress Control Number: 2021940658

Cover and book design by Kylie Alexander for Page Street Publishing Co.
Photography by Becky Winkler

Printed and bound in the United States of America

Page Street Publishing protects our planet by donating to nonprofits like The Trustees, which focuses on local land conservation.

We dedicate this book to our wonderful children,
Riley, Marsel and Jada. We hope we have made you
all proud. We love you and thank you for motivating us
to strive for more and to achieve our goals.

TABLE OF CONTENTS

INTRODUCTION

Never in a million years did we imagine that we would be writing a cookbook from scratch that builds upon the success of our Noodle Worship brand. But here we are! We could not be more honored, excited and humbled to present this collection of recipes to all of the other noodle worshippers around the world and to our supporters.

We are Larone and Tiffani Thompson from Los Angeles, California, and we are the creators of @noodleworship, most famous on Instagram, where we share videos and photographs of the best, most craveable noodle dishes from around the world. Our wild journey towards our social media account—and this book—has a pretty unconventional backstory that begins with two bowls of ramen. We used to think ramen meant boiling some dried noodles, opening a seasoning packet and calling it a day. We might have been on the late train in that respect, but we have more than made up for lost time since then. Our noodle obsession has moved from Japanese ramen to Korean jjapaguri to Italian classics such as Cacio e Pepe (page 19) to hearty casseroles like Cheesy Baked Mostaccioli (page 106) and to refreshing, healthy pasta salads loaded with crisp vegetables.

After discovering all the glory that noodles could provide, we decided to create a social media account where we can display beautiful content to people all over the world who love noodles as much as we do. In the process, we unwittingly fostered a community of like-minded noodle-heads. In the six years that followed, that community blossomed into hundreds of thousands of followers.

Our @noodleworship brand was a hit from its inception in 2016. Alongside our own personal dining journey throughout California, we displayed international content. It was only a matter of time before the requests for recipes began to pile up. And before long, we had the initial spark for this cookbook. In the end, we selected the recipes that our fan base requested the most, added some of our own personal favorites and tossed in some creative spins as well.

We are a family of four (soon to be five), so free time is definitely not our friend. Our mission with this book is to provide simple, straightforward and flavorful recipes for the noodles and pasta you all love that don't require hours to make—with the added focus of making them family friendly. We pledge that these dishes are easy enough for beginner cooks yet delicious enough to satisfy true home chefs.

So please, take a dive into this cookbook and discover what all the hype is about, and hopefully—if not already—you too will become a noodle worshipper like us. And thanks to all for your continuous love, support and encouragement.

Larone and Tiffani Thompson

ITALIAN—
INSPIRED
PASTA

Italian food is one of the most celebrated cuisines in the world, with much of the focus on pasta. When it comes to life's most simple yet satisfying pleasures, it's nearly impossible to top Italian noodle dishes. And judging by the reactions we get on our social media accounts, other noodle worshippers definitely agree.

What makes pasta so special, in our opinion, is the near-limitless variety when it comes to noodles and sauce. Pairing a particular pasta shape with this topping or that one is half the fun. Many of the recipes in this chapter are simple and made with just a handful of staple ingredients to be as true to their authentic origins as possible. That's why it's so important to use the best quality ingredients you can find and afford. This applies to things like olive oil, aged cheeses, canned tomatoes and imported meats like prosciutto.

Some of our family favorites include classics like Cacio e Pepe (page 19), Spaghetti Carbonara (page 40) and Hearty Rigatoni Bolognese (page 27). We also created some new favorites like Fettucine Alfredo with Seared Scallops (page 28) and Pesto Gnocchi with Burrata & Crispy Prosciutto (page 23). Whenever we are looking for something quick and delicious to make that the entire family will enjoy, very often it will be one of the dishes from this chapter. We hope that you and your family will love them as much as we do.

SPICY RIGATONI VODKA

If you've ever ordered and enjoyed pasta with vodka cream sauce at an Italian restaurant, we think you'll definitely want to make this recipe at home. It's surprisingly easy and the results are decadent! It's hard to pinpoint exactly what vodka—being an odorless, largely flavorless spirit—brings to this recipe, but we can assure you that it does make a big difference in the final dish. Maybe it's the subtle heat and bite of the alcohol, which balances out the sweetness of the tomatoes, that makes this iconic Italian pasta so perfect. For this book, we wanted to honor the traditional recipe as closely as possible, but we did add Calabrian chili peppers because we love the fruity spice they bring to the table.

Serves 4

12 oz (340 g) dried rigatoni

1½ tbsp (22 ml) extra-virgin olive oil

3 tbsp (42 g) butter

1 small onion, finely chopped

4 oz (113 g) diced pancetta

1½ tsp (4 g) minced garlic

3 tbsp (28 g) chopped Calabrian chili peppers (jarred is fine)

½ cup (120 ml) vodka

½ cup (132 g) tomato paste

1¼ cups (300 ml) heavy cream

Kosher salt and black pepper to taste

Grated Parmesan cheese to taste, for garnish

4 tsp (3 g) finely chopped fresh basil, for garnish

Bring a large pot of salted water to boil over high heat. Add the pasta and cook until al dente, stirring occasionally, according to the package directions. Scoop out and reserve 1 cup (240 ml) of the pasta water before draining the pasta.

Meanwhile, place a large skillet over medium-high heat and warm the olive oil and butter. When the butter has melted, add the onion and pancetta and cook, stirring occasionally, until the onion has softened, about 5 minutes. Add the garlic and chili peppers and cook for 1 minute. Add the vodka and cook for 30 seconds. Remove from the heat, add the tomato paste and stir until well blended. Return the skillet to medium-low heat, add the cream and bring the sauce to a gentle simmer. Season to taste with salt and pepper.

Add the cooked pasta and ½ cup (120 ml) of reserved pasta water and stir to combine. If the sauce appears too thick, add more of the reserved pasta water by the tablespoon (15 ml), while stirring, until it reaches the desired consistency.

Divide the pasta among four bowls, then top with the Parmesan and basil before serving.

BIG FAT SHELLS

We call these flavor bombs "Italian burritos." Each big, fat shell is like a mini-lasagna, complete with pasta, cheese and sauce. We think the addition of zesty sausage makes a huge difference, adding a little something special in every bite. If you enjoy spicy foods, go ahead and swap the sweet Italian sausage for one of the spicier varieties. The panko breadcrumb topping adds a nice texture. We think this dish is super impressive straight out of the oven.

Serves 4

2 tbsp (36 g) plus a pinch of kosher salt, divided

16 dried jumbo pasta shells

8 oz (226 g) ground sweet Italian sausage

1 egg

1⅓ cups (328 g) ricotta cheese

2 cups (225 g) shredded mozzarella cheese, divided

⅓ cup (33 g) grated Parmesan cheese

1¼ tsp (2 g) Italian seasoning

Pinch of black pepper

2½ cups (600 ml) jarred marinara, divided (we like Rao's Homemade brand)

½ cup (28 g) panko breadcrumbs

1 tbsp (4 g) chopped fresh parsley, for garnish

Preheat the oven to 375°F (190°C).

To a large pot of water, add 2 tablespoons (36 g) of salt and bring to a boil over high heat. Add the shells and cook until al dente, stirring occasionally, according to the package directions. Drain, rinse with cold water, drain again and set aside (see the Note below for tips).

Place a large skillet over medium-high heat. Cook the sausage, breaking the meat apart with a wooden spoon, until nicely browned, about 10 minutes. Drain and set aside.

In a large mixing bowl, whisk together the egg, ricotta, 1 cup (112 g) of the mozzarella, the Parmesan, Italian seasoning, and a pinch each of kosher salt and pepper. Add the cooked sausage and stir to combine.

Grease a 9 x 13-inch (23 x 33-cm) baking dish with nonstick cooking spray. Pour in 1½ cups (360 ml) of the marinara and spread it evenly across the bottom. Stuff each shell with the filling and arrange them open-side up in the baking pan. Spoon the remaining marinara over the shells. Top with the remaining mozzarella. Evenly sprinkle the breadcrumbs over the top.

Cover the pan tightly with aluminum foil and cook for 20 minutes. Remove the foil and continue cooking until the cheese is completely melted, about 10 minutes. Top with the chopped parsley.

Note: Our cooking tips for working with shells are to cook them to al dente (or the lowest number for the cook time range given on the package instructions), not any longer or the shells will break easily while stuffing. Drain the shells in a colander and rinse them under cold running water until they're completely cooled, then drain them thoroughly; this makes them easier to handle.

TUSCAN SHRIMP PASTA

If we see shrimp in a recipe, chances are good we're going to give it a whirl! This one is over-the-top delicious, so it immediately earned a spot in this book. The shrimp are bathed in a creamy, cheesy, garlicky sauce that is fortified with fresh spinach and sweet sun-dried tomatoes. When making this dish, you want a pasta shape that grabs and holds every last drop of this decadent sauce, so that means something with plenty of ridges and valleys, like rotini.

Serves 4–6

10 oz (282 g) dried rotini

2 tbsp (28 g) butter

1 lb (454 g) medium to large shrimp, peeled and deveined (you can leave the tails on or peel off)

Kosher salt and black pepper to preference

3 garlic cloves, minced

1 cup (240 ml) heavy cream

1 tsp sweet paprika

1 tsp Italian seasoning

¼ cup (25 g) freshly grated Parmesan cheese

½ cup (27 g) jarred oil-packed sun-dried tomatoes, chopped

1 cup (30 g) chopped baby spinach

Bring a large pot of salted water to a boil over high heat. Add the pasta and cook until al dente, stirring occasionally, according to the package directions. Drain and set aside.

Meanwhile, place a large skillet over medium heat and warm the butter. When the butter has melted, add the shrimp, season to your preference with salt and pepper and cook until opaque, 2½ minutes per side. Transfer the shrimp to a plate.

In the same skillet, cook the garlic for 30 seconds, until fragrant. Add the cream, paprika and Italian seasoning and stir to blend. Add the Parmesan and stir until melted and smooth. Reduce the heat to low, stir in the sun-dried tomatoes and simmer for 2 minutes. Add the spinach and cook until wilted, about 2 minutes. Add the drained pasta and shrimp and cook for 1 minute to warm them through.

Plate and serve immediately.

RED PESTO RIGATONI

While researching and writing this cookbook, we discovered tons of different twists on pesto. When it comes to variations on the classic recipe featuring basil, pine nuts, garlic, Parmesan and olive oil, the possibilities are limitless! By adjusting the quantities of ingredients, adding in different ones and replacing others with something else entirely, you can create exciting new flavors, colors and textures. This recipe turns a vibrant red thanks to the sun-dried tomatoes and roasted red bell peppers, which also add a pleasant earthiness to the final dish. We prefer to use jarred sun-dried tomatoes and roasted peppers, and we scoop these from their jars with a spoon, including any liquid that collects on each spoonful. We think rigatoni is the perfect pasta for this sauce, but feel free to experiment.

Serves 4

10 oz (283 g) dried rigatoni

1 cup (54 g) jarred oil-packed sun-dried tomatoes

1 cup (130 g) jarred roasted red bell peppers

1 cup (24 g) fresh basil leaves

¼ cup (34 g) pine nuts

¾ cup (75 g) grated Parmesan cheese

2 tbsp (30 ml) lemon juice

1 garlic clove, minced

¼ tsp kosher salt

½ cup (120 ml) extra-virgin olive oil

Bring a large pot of salted water to a boil over high heat. Add the pasta and cook until al dente, stirring occasionally, according to the package directions. Scoop out and reserve 1 cup (240 ml) of the pasta water before draining the pasta and returning it to the pot.

Meanwhile, in a food processor or blender, place the sun-dried tomatoes, bell peppers, basil, pine nuts, Parmesan, lemon juice, garlic and salt and pulse about 10 times. With the machine running, slowly add the olive oil. Process until smooth, making sure to scrape down the sides a few times, about 30 seconds.

Slowly add the red pesto to the pasta until you reach your desired amount. You may not need all of the pesto; any leftovers can be stored in the fridge for up to a week. Add the reserved pasta water to the sauce by the tablespoon (15 ml), while stirring, until the sauce reaches your desired consistency.

CACIO E PEPE

When a server at an Italian restaurant recommended this dish to us, it was love at first bite. Since then, we've been on a quest not only to find the best restaurant versions of this famous pasta, but also to create a recipe for people to prepare and enjoy at home. Because there literally are just four ingredients—well, and a little water—this recipe leans heavy on technique. Don't worry, we lay it all out step-by-step so you won't suffer the same mistakes that we did early on. The most challenging part is getting the consistency of the cheese sauce just right: thick enough to stick to the noodles, but not clumpy. The key is to add the water in small amounts—you can always add more, but you can't take any away. Also, we think this dish is a million times better with fresh-cracked black pepper so you really get that "kick."

Serves 4

2 tbsp (36 g) kosher salt

12 oz (340 g) dried bucatini or spaghetti

2 tsp (4 g) fresh-cracked black pepper, plus more for serving

1½ cups (150 g) freshly grated Pecorino Romano or Parmesan cheese, plus more for serving

To a large pot of water, add the salt and bring to a boil over high heat. Add the pasta and cook, stirring occasionally, until al dente, for about 2 minutes less than the package directions.

Meanwhile, in a large skillet over medium heat, cook the black pepper while shaking the pan, until aromatic, about 2 minutes. Remove from the heat.

When the pasta is almost done, remove ½ cup (120 ml) of the pasta water and add it to the skillet containing the black pepper and return the skillet to a high heat. Place the Pecorino Romano in a large bowl, add another ½ cup (120 ml) of the hot pasta water, and blend with a silicone spatula until creamy and smooth. If the sauce appears too thick, continue adding pasta water by the tablespoon (15 ml), while stirring, until it reaches the desired consistency.

When the pasta is done, transfer it with tongs directly from the water to the skillet with the black pepper and continue cooking until just tender, about 2 minutes. Remove from the heat, add the cheese sauce, and stir to blend. If the sauce appears too thick, stir in another tablespoon or two (15 or 30 ml) of the pasta water. Taste and adjust the seasoning, adding more black pepper if desired.

Plate immediately and top with more freshly grated cheese and black pepper.

FRIED RAVIOLI WITH CHUNKY MARINARA

If you love regular ravioli like we do, then you're going to go crazy for this version. When you deep-fry ravioli, you wind up with two completely different textures in one bite: the crispy-crunchy shell followed by the creamy, gooey interior. That contrast is what makes this recipe really stand out in our minds. You can use fresh or frozen ravioli with whatever filling you prefer, but we think classic cheese is the best. And because you absolutely must have a dipping sauce, we provided a recipe for a simple but flavorful marinara. We kept it rustic and chunky and also added some heavy cream for a rich and creamy touch. These fried ravioli make a great snack for entertaining.

Serves 4

CHUNKY MARINARA

2 tbsp (30 ml) olive oil

1 medium yellow onion, diced

4 garlic cloves, minced

5 tomatoes, roughly chopped

¼ tsp crushed red pepper flakes

1 tsp dried oregano

1 tbsp (3 g) chopped fresh basil

½ tsp kosher salt

¼ tsp black pepper

½ cup (120 ml) heavy cream

FRIED RAVIOLI

2 eggs

⅓ cup (80 ml) whole milk

1¾ cups (189 g) Italian breadcrumbs

¼ cup (25 g) grated Parmesan cheese

20 cheese ravioli (refrigerated or frozen and thawed)

2 quarts (1.9 L) vegetable oil or peanut oil

Kosher salt

To make the marinara, place a large saucepan over medium-high heat and warm the olive oil. When the oil is hot, add the onion and cook until softened, about 5 minutes. Add the garlic and cook, stirring frequently, until aromatic, about 2 minutes. Add the tomatoes, red pepper flakes, oregano, basil, salt and pepper and bring to a simmer. Reduce the heat to maintain a gentle simmer, cover and cook, stirring occasionally, for 25 minutes. Stir in the heavy cream and continue simmering for 5 minutes. Remove from the heat.

To make the fried ravioli, in a shallow bowl, place the eggs and milk and beat to combine. In a separate shallow bowl, place the breadcrumbs and Parmesan and stir to combine. Working with one ravioli at a time, dip it in the egg and milk mixture, allowing the excess to drip off. Then, dredge it in the breadcrumbs, making sure it's evenly coated, and place it on a plate. Repeat with the remaining ravioli.

Into a tabletop fryer or a large, heavy pot over medium-high heat, pour the vegetable oil. Heat to 350°F (175°C). Cover a large sheet pan with paper towels. Working in batches, carefully lower the ravioli into the hot oil and fry until golden brown, about 3 minutes. Use a slotted spoon to remove the ravioli onto the paper towel-lined sheet pan to drain. Season the ravioli with salt immediately after removing them from the oil.

Serve with the chunky marinara for dipping.

PESTO GNOCCHI WITH BURRATA & CRISPY PROSCIUTTO

This recipe combines three of our absolute favorite foods into one over-the-top dish. We are huge fans of gnocchi because of their light, pillowy texture. And we think there is no better sauce for gnocchi than pesto because of the way it sticks to the pasta, not to mention the intense basil and garlic flavor that it brings to the party. But what carries this recipe across the finish line is the Burrata, a creamy cheese that oozes into the pasta and enriches the sauce. The proverbial cherry on top is the crispy fried prosciutto chips. You can find fresh Burrata at most Italian markets, but it's increasingly available in the cheese section at conventional grocery stores. Look for the larger 4-ounce (113-g) balls—you'll thank us.

Serves 4

4 cups (96 g) fresh basil leaves

4 garlic cloves, roughly chopped

½ cup (68 g) pine nuts

1 cup (100 g) grated Parmesan cheese

¼ tsp kosher salt

Juice of 2 lemons

1 cup (240 ml) extra-virgin olive oil

1 lb (454 g) gnocchi

2 oz (57 g) prosciutto, diced

4 (4-oz [113-g]) balls of Burrata, for garnish

In a food processor or blender, combine the basil, garlic, pine nuts, Parmesan, salt and lemon juice and pulse about 10 times, making sure to scrape down the sides a few times. While the machine is running, add the oil in a slow, steady stream. Continue blending until thoroughly combined, about 30 seconds.

Bring a large pot of salted water to a boil over high heat. Add the gnocchi and cook until al dente, stirring occasionally, according to the package directions. Scoop out and reserve ½ cup (120 ml) of the gnocchi water before draining the gnocchi.

Meanwhile, place a small skillet over medium-high heat. Cook the prosciutto, stirring occasionally, until golden brown and crisp, about 5 minutes. Remove to a paper towel-lined plate to drain.

Return the drained gnocchi to the large pot, add the pesto and stir to combine. If the sauce appears too thick, add the reserved pasta water by the tablespoon (15 ml) while stirring, until it reaches the desired consistency.

Divide the gnocchi among four bowls, top each with a ball of Burrata and garnish with some of the crispy prosciutto.

ORECCHIETTE WITH BACON, KALE & SUN-DRIED TOMATOES

To us, this recipe just looks, feels and tastes like autumn on a plate. The smokiness from the bacon (and bacon drippings) combined with hearty, seasonal kale creates a robust, satisfying and flavorful dinner. We chose orecchiette because it's a dense, firm and pleasantly chewy pasta that can stand up to the other ingredients. This recipe is a great example of how a little bit of the reserved pasta water is all it takes to transform an otherwise sauce-less pasta into a silky, rich finished product.

Serves 4

12 oz (340 g) dried orecchiette

6 cups (402 g) chopped fresh or frozen kale leaves

3 slices bacon, diced

4 tsp (11 g) minced garlic

½ cup (27 g) jarred sun-dried tomatoes, thinly sliced

¾ tsp crushed red pepper flakes

4 tbsp (25 g) freshly grated Parmesan cheese, for garnish

Bring a large pot of salted water to a boil over high heat. Add the pasta and cook until al dente, stirring occasionally, according to the package directions. When there are 2 minutes remaining in the cook time, add the kale. Scoop out and reserve ½ cup (120 ml) of the pasta water before draining the pasta and kale.

Meanwhile, place a large skillet over medium-high heat. Cook the bacon, stirring occasionally, until crisp, about 5 minutes. Transfer to a paper towel-lined plate to drain, leaving the rendered fat in the skillet.

Reduce the skillet's heat to medium-low and cook the garlic, sun-dried tomatoes and red pepper flakes, stirring constantly, for 30 seconds. Add the pasta, kale and reserved pasta water and cook, while stirring, for 1 minute.

Remove from the heat and top with the Parmesan and bacon before serving.

HEARTY RIGATONI BOLOGNESE

A good Bolognese is a hearty, satisfying meat sauce, and that was our aim in developing our version of this classic. It would go great with any pasta, but we think rigatoni is the best because the large tubes fill up with sauce. We let this sauce cook low and slow for about 2 hours. Set a timer to go off every 20 minutes or so to remind yourself to give the sauce a stir so it doesn't burn and to keep an eye on the liquid level. Don't be intimidated by the long-ish list of ingredients. Once you gather and measure out all the components, it is not at all complicated. And the results are totally worth it. This dish is another family favorite.

Serves 4

1 small yellow onion, roughly chopped

1 small carrot, roughly chopped

1 celery stalk, roughly chopped

2 tbsp (30 ml) extra-virgin olive oil

4 oz (113 g) pancetta, finely chopped

1 lb (454 g) ground beef (80/20)

2 garlic cloves, minced

1 cup (240 ml) dry white wine

2 tbsp (32 g) tomato paste

2¼ cups (540 g) tomato puree

Pinch of nutmeg

1 bay leaf

2 tbsp (36 g) plus a pinch of kosher salt

1 cup (240 ml) whole milk

1 lb (454 g) dried rigatoni

½ cup (50 g) grated Parmesan cheese, plus more for serving

Place the onion, carrot and celery in a food processor or blender and pulse until very finely chopped, making sure to scrape down the sides a few times.

Place a large saucepan over medium heat and warm the olive oil. When the oil is hot, add the pancetta and cook until browned, about 5 minutes. Add the chopped vegetable mixture and cook, stirring occasionally, until the vegetables have softened, about 8 minutes. Add the ground beef and garlic and cook, breaking the meat apart with a wooden spoon, until nicely browned, about 8 minutes. Add the wine, increase the heat to high and cook until most of the liquid has evaporated, 2 to 4 minutes.

Reduce the heat to low, add the tomato paste, tomato puree, nutmeg, bay leaf and a pinch of salt, stirring well to fully combine. Cover and cook, stirring occasionally, for about 2 hours. Periodically check to make sure there's enough liquid in the saucepan to prevent scorching. If it appears dry, add a few tablespoons (about 45 ml) of water.

After 2 hours, remove the bay leaf, stir in the milk and continue cooking for 15 minutes. Remove the sauce from the heat.

Meanwhile, to a large pot of water add 2 tablespoons (36 g) of the salt and bring to a boil over high heat. Add the pasta and cook until al dente, stirring occasionally, according to the package directions. Scoop out and reserve 1 cup (240 ml) of the pasta water before draining the pasta.

Add the drained pasta, Parmesan and some of the reserved pasta water to the sauce and stir for 1 minute. Add more of the pasta water until you get a consistency that you like.

Serve with additional Parmesan cheese.

FETTUCCINE ALFREDO WITH SEARED SCALLOPS

I'm sure we're not the only ones who can't get enough fettuccine Alfredo. It's a dish that both of us have been enjoying for years and years. Many restaurants prepare this classic pasta with chicken, but we always look for ways to sneak in more seafood. Because we have never seen the dish prepared with scallops, we decided to mix the two together and were blown away by the results! This recipe also works great with large shrimp (shelled and deveined) in place of the scallops. We knew that if we ever got around to writing a cookbook, this recipe would be one of the headliners. Warning: This dish is hard to stop eating, so proceed with caution!

Serves 4

ALFREDO SAUCE

½ cup (114 g) salted butter

1½ cups (360 ml) heavy whipping cream

2 tsp (6 g) minced garlic

½ tsp Italian seasoning

2 tbsp (36 g) plus ½ tsp kosher salt, divided

¼ tsp black pepper

2 cups (200 g) freshly grated Parmesan cheese

12 oz (340 g) dried fettuccine

SCALLOPS

1 lb (454 g) scallops

Kosher salt and black pepper

2 tbsp (30 ml) extra-virgin olive oil

3 tbsp (42 g) unsalted butter

2 tbsp (30 ml) fresh lemon juice

1½ tbsp (13 g) minced garlic

To make the Alfredo sauce, place a large skillet over low heat, and warm the butter and cream for 2 minutes, until the butter is melted. Add the garlic, Italian seasoning, ½ teaspoon of salt and pepper and cook, while whisking, for 1 minute. Add the Parmesan and whisk until completely melted and smooth. Turn off the heat.

In a large pot of water, add 2 tablespoons (36 g) of salt and bring to a boil over high heat. Add the pasta and cook, stirring occasionally, until al dente according to the package instructions. When the pasta is done, scoop out and reserve 1 cup (240 ml) of the pasta water before draining the pasta.

Return the Alfredo sauce to medium-low heat. Transfer the pasta to the sauce and gently toss to blend and heat through. If the sauce appears too thick, add the reserved pasta water by the tablespoon (15 ml), while stirring, until it reaches the desired consistency. Keep warm over very low heat while you cook the scallops.

To make the scallops, use paper towels to pat them dry on both sides. Season both sides of the scallops with salt and pepper. Place a large skillet over high heat and warm the olive oil. When the oil is very hot, add the scallops in a single layer and cook, without disturbing, until golden brown, about 3 minutes. Flip and continue cooking until the second side is golden brown and the scallops are cooked through, about 2 minutes. Transfer to a plate.

Reduce the heat to medium-low and wait 1 minute for the pan to cool slightly, then warm the butter. When the butter has melted, add the lemon juice and garlic. Cook, while stirring, for 1 minute. Pour the sauce over the cooked scallops.

To serve, divide the pasta among four bowls and top with the scallops.

LEMON PESTO FARFALLE

We love pesto and we love lemon, so we decided to combine the two flavors even though it's not the traditional thing to do. Other than the addition of fresh lemon juice, this recipe features a pretty classic pesto sauce. Farfalle—also referred to as bowtie pasta—is the perfect noodle for this recipe because the little ruffles grab and hold the sauce perfectly. If you want to swap out the pine nuts for more budget-friendly walnuts, go ahead because the results are great either way. Also, to tone down the basil flavor, you can substitute spinach leaves for some of the fresh basil. If you feel like making a double batch of this pesto, it keeps great in the fridge for up to a week. Not only do we love this dish, but so too does our two-year-old son, and that's the biggest compliment we can receive!

Serves 4

2 tbsp (36 g) plus ¼ tsp kosher salt, divided

1 lb (454 g) dried farfalle

4 cups (96 g) fresh basil leaves

½ cup (68 g) pine nuts

1 cup (100 g) grated Parmesan cheese, plus more for serving

Juice of 2 lemons

4 garlic cloves

1 cup (240 ml) extra-virgin olive oil

To a large pot of water, add 2 tablespoons (36 g) of salt and bring to a boil over high heat. Add the pasta and cook, stirring occasionally, until al dente, about 1 minute less than the package directions.

Meanwhile, in a food processor or blender, place the basil, pine nuts, Parmesan, lemon juice, garlic and the remaining ¼ teaspoon of salt and pulse about 10 times. While the machine is running, add the olive oil in a slow, steady stream. Process until smooth, making sure to scrape down the sides a few times, about 1 minute.

When the pasta is almost done cooking, begin heating a large skillet over medium-high heat. Scoop out and reserve ½ cup (120 ml) of the pasta water. Drain the pasta and place it in the skillet along with ¼ cup (60 ml) of the reserved pasta water. Add the pesto to the skillet and stir to combine it with the pasta. Cook for about 2 minutes, stirring constantly, or until the pasta has finished cooking to your liking. If the sauce appears too thick, add more of the reserved pasta water by the tablespoon (15 ml), while stirring, until it reaches the desired consistency.

Transfer the pasta to plates and top with additional grated Parmesan.

SHRIMP SCAMPI LINGUINE

It's difficult to improve upon shrimp scampi, a time-tested classic that features sweet seafood in a lemony butter and garlic sauce. It is one of those unforgettable dishes that also happens to be remarkably straightforward in its preparation. For this recipe, we toss those dreamy crustaceans with linguine to stretch out the dish. Paired with a salad and some crusty Italian bread, it makes for an elegant weekend—or weekday—meal. The ingredients below call for tail-on shrimp because we think they enhance the presentation, but feel free to use fully peeled, tail-off shrimp if that's what you prefer or have on hand.

Serves 4

12 oz (340 g) dried linguine

3½ tbsp (50 g) unsalted butter

2½ tbsp (38 ml) extra-virgin olive oil

4 tsp (11 g) minced garlic

½ tbsp (2 g) crushed red pepper flakes

½ cup (120 ml) dry white wine

1 lb (454 g) tail-on shrimp, peeled and deveined

Kosher salt and black pepper to taste

2 tbsp (30 ml) fresh lemon juice

¼ cup (15 g) chopped fresh parsley

Bring a large pot of salted water to a boil over high heat. Add the pasta and cook until al dente, stirring occasionally, according to the package directions. Drain the pasta and set aside.

Meanwhile, place a large skillet over medium heat and warm the butter and olive oil. When the butter has melted, add the garlic and cook, stirring constantly, for 1 minute. Add the red pepper flakes and wine and cook until the liquid reduces by half, about 2 minutes. Add the shrimp and cook until opaque, 2 minutes per side. Season to taste with salt and pepper. Add the lemon juice, parsley and drained pasta and toss to combine.

SPINACH ALFREDO RADIATORI

Out of all the amazing pasta shapes in the world, radiatori might be our favorite. If the name sounds like "radiator" that's no coincidence because that's kind of what they like. In addition to being cool to look at, the pleats in the pasta are great at grabbing and holding on to sauces like the creamy Alfredo in this recipe. We balance the rich, cheesy sauce with a healthy addition of fresh spinach. Make sure to use freshly grated Parmesan or you may run into clumping issues when making the sauce with the pre-shredded type.

Serves 4

10 oz (283 g) dried radiatori

½ cup (114 g) butter

1½ cups (360 ml) heavy whipping cream

1 cup (30 g) chopped fresh spinach leaves

2 tsp (6 g) minced garlic

½ tsp Italian seasoning

½ tsp kosher salt

¼ tsp black pepper

2 cups (200 g) freshly grated Parmesan cheese

Bring a large pot of salted water to a boil over high heat. Add the pasta and cook until al dente, stirring occasionally, according to the package directions. Scoop out and reserve 1 cup (240 ml) of the pasta water before draining the pasta.

Meanwhile, place a large skillet over medium heat and warm the butter and cream. When the butter has melted, add the spinach. Reduce the heat to low and cook for 2 minutes. Add the garlic, Italian seasoning, salt and pepper and cook, while stirring, for 1 minute. Working with a handful at a time, add the Parmesan and stir until completely melted and smooth. Add the drained pasta and stir to combine. If the sauce appears too thick, add the reserved pasta water by the tablespoon (15 ml), while stirring, until it reaches the desired consistency.

CAVATAPPI & PROSCIUTTO

This recipe might look simple (because it is), but don't let that fool you; the finished dish bursts with classic Italian flavors. This is one of those times when every ingredient matters, so don't omit anything and be sure to opt for the freshest, best-quality ingredients you can find. That means extra-virgin olive oil, imported Italian prosciutto, fresh flat-leaf parsley and aged Parmigiano-Reggiano. Instead of grating the cheese, we prefer to shave it into long shingles with a vegetable peeler. That way it doesn't melt into the pasta immediately and get all gooey, and instead provides more of that bold flavor in each bite.

Serves 4

12 oz (340 g) dried cavatappi

1½ tsp (7 g) butter

1½ tsp (4 g) minced garlic

3 tbsp (45 ml) extra-virgin olive oil

4 oz (113 g) prosciutto, chopped

1½ tbsp (6 g) chopped fresh parsley

¼ tsp black pepper

½ cup (50 g) shaved Parmigiano-Reggiano, for garnish

Bring a large pot of salted water to a boil over high heat. Add the pasta and cook until al dente, stirring occasionally, according to the package directions. Scoop out and reserve ¼ cup (60 ml) of the pasta water before draining the pasta.

Place a large skillet over medium heat and warm the butter. When the butter has melted, add the garlic and cook for 30 seconds, until fragrant. Remove from the heat.

When the pasta is done, use a slotted spoon to transfer it directly from the water to the skillet along with the reserved pasta water. Toss or stir to combine with the garlic butter. Add the olive oil, prosciutto, parsley and black pepper and stir to blend.

Garnish with the shaved Parmigiano-Reggiano.

PESTO ALLA TRAPANESE FARFALLE

What happens when you blend tomatoes into a classic pesto sauce? You end up with this famous—and delicious—dish from Sicily. The tomatoes transform the normally thick paste into a looser sauce that perfectly coats the pasta. Of course, the riper and sweeter the tomatoes, the better the end results. We love this with cherry tomatoes, but you could use the same weight of other types of in-season tomatoes; just roughly chop them into pieces. Because the sauce doesn't get cooked (only warmed by the cooked pasta), that summer sweetness is preserved in the final dish. We love the nutty flavor that the almonds provide, but if you want to stick with the traditional pine nuts, that's great too.

Serves 4

½ cup (54 g) slivered almonds

1 tsp minced garlic

1¾ cups (262 g) cherry tomatoes

1 cup (24 g) fresh basil

½ cup (50 g) freshly grated Parmesan cheese

¼ tsp lemon juice

1 tsp kosher salt

¼ tsp ground pepper

½ cup (120 ml) extra-virgin olive oil

8 oz (226 g) dried farfalle

In a food processor or blender, place the almonds and garlic and pulse until finely chopped. Add the tomatoes, basil, Parmesan, lemon juice, salt and pepper and pulse until finely chopped, making sure to scrape down the sides a few times. With the machine running, slowly add the olive oil. Process until smooth, occasionally scraping down the sides, about 1 minute. Set aside for the flavors to meld while you cook the pasta.

Bring a large pot of salted water to a boil over high heat. Add the pasta and cook until al dente, stirring occasionally, according to the package directions. Drain the pasta and return it to the pot. Add the pesto and stir to blend.

SPAGHETTI CARBONARA

This famous Italian pasta is delicious proof that with the right technique you can transform a few modest ingredients into a dish of pure luxury. Done well, carbonara is rich, silky, salty and creamy—despite the fact that there is zero cream in the recipe. Done wrong and you end up with a clumpy, gluey mess. The key is to combine the pasta and egg mixture off the stove so that the heat of the pasta gently cooks the eggs. It helps to start with room temperature eggs. Also, when the ingredients are this few, every single one counts; that means use real Italian Parmigiano-Reggiano cheese, freshly grated black pepper and good-quality pancetta. If you can't get pancetta, bacon will do in a pinch.

Serves 4–6

8 oz (226 g) pancetta, diced

12 oz (340 g) dried spaghetti

1 egg, at room temperature

3 egg yolks, at room temperature

½ tsp freshly ground black pepper

8 tbsp (50 g) freshly grated Parmigiano-Reggiano, divided

In a large skillet over medium-high heat, cook the pancetta, stirring frequently, until lightly crisp and golden brown, about 8 minutes. Transfer to a paper towel-lined plate to drain, leaving the rendered fat in the skillet.

Meanwhile, bring a large pot of salted water to a boil over high heat. Add the pasta and cook until al dente, stirring occasionally, according to the package directions. Scoop out and reserve 1 cup (240 ml) of the pasta water before draining the pasta.

In a large mixing bowl, whisk the egg and the egg yolks until completely blended. Add the black pepper and 6 tablespoons (38 g) of Parmigiano-Reggiano and whisk to combine.

Return the skillet to medium-high heat. When the rendered fat is hot, add the drained pasta. Heat, tossing or stirring, for 1 minute. Remove the skillet from the heat, immediately pour in the egg and cheese mixture and toss until the noodles are completely coated. Add the reserved pasta water by the tablespoon (15 ml), while stirring, until it reaches a creamy consistency. Stir in the pancetta.

Divide the pasta among four bowls and top with the remaining 2 tablespoons (12 g) of Parmigiano-Reggiano.

SPAGHETTI AGLIO E OLIO

As busy working parents, there are days when it's all we can do to get a meal together and on the table in time for supper. It is precisely those nights that we dig into the well of classic Italian dishes. A quick scan of the ingredients list reveals just a handful of items—and most, if not all, are staples that most home cooks have sitting around in the cupboard or pantry. This recipe comes together in such a flavorful, elegant way that it still surprises us when we make it. The trick is to hold back some of the starchy pasta-cooking water to help build the sauce. Because there are so few components to this dish, it's important to use fresh ingredients: fresh garlic, fresh parsley and freshly grated cheese.

Serves 4

12 oz (340 g) dried spaghetti

⅓ cup plus 2 tsp (90 ml) extra-virgin olive oil

5 garlic cloves, thinly sliced

½ tsp crushed red pepper flakes

2 tbsp (8 g) finely chopped fresh parsley

Freshly grated Parmesan cheese, for garnish

Bring a large pot of salted water to a boil over high heat. Add the spaghetti and cook until al dente, stirring occasionally, according to the package directions. Scoop out and reserve ½ cup (120 ml) of the pasta water before draining the pasta.

Meanwhile, place a large saucepan over medium-high heat and warm the olive oil. When the oil is hot, add the garlic and red pepper flakes and cook, stirring frequently, until the garlic is fragrant and golden brown, about 3 minutes. Be careful not to burn the garlic. Reduce the heat to low.

Transfer the drained pasta to the saucepan along with ¼ cup (60 ml) of the reserved pasta water. Stir well to evenly coat the pasta in the sauce. If the sauce appears too dry, add more of the reserved pasta water by the tablespoon (15 ml), while stirring, until it reaches the desired consistency. Remove from the heat and stir in the parsley.

Divide the pasta among four bowls and top with the Parmesan cheese.

CALAMARATA PASTA WITH CALAMARI & TOMATOES

If you love seafood as much as we do, then you will definitely want to give this recipe a try. If you are unfamiliar with it, calamarata pasta gets its name because it resembles calamari rings, so the pairing of the two is a natural one. The seafood gets a sweet boost from two types of tomatoes, a slight kick from red pepper flakes and a healthy dose of garlic. If you can find fresh calamari—and are comfortable cleaning it and breaking it down—by all means, go that route. But we think that frozen (and thawed) calamari works great in this recipe. For those of you who are squeamish about the tentacles, feel free to omit them if you wish; it won't affect the overall flavor at all.

Serves 4

6 whole calamari (thawed if frozen)

12 oz (340 g) dried calamarata

4 tbsp (60 ml) extra-virgin olive oil

¼ tsp crushed red pepper flakes

2 tsp (6 g) minced garlic

4 tbsp (16 g) chopped fresh parsley, divided

¾ cup (180 ml) dry white wine

1 tbsp (16 g) double-concentrated tomato paste

8 oz (226 g) cherry tomatoes, halved

Pinch of kosher salt

If the calamari tentacles are attached to the bodies, separate them with a knife. Slice the bodies into thick rings that are the approximate shape of the pasta.

Bring a large pot of salted water to a boil over high heat. Add the pasta and cook until al dente, stirring occasionally, according to the package directions. Scoop out and reserve ½ cup (120 ml) of the pasta water before draining the pasta.

Place a large skillet over medium heat. Cook the olive oil, red pepper flakes, garlic, 3 tablespoons (12 g) of parsley and the calamari tubes and tentacles (if using), while stirring, until the garlic begins to brown, about 2 minutes. Add the white wine and tomato paste and cook, while stirring, until the liquid is reduced by half, about 5 minutes. Add the tomatoes and salt, reduce the heat to low and cook, stirring occasionally, for 6 minutes.

Add the drained pasta and the remaining 1 tablespoon (4 g) of parsley and cook, while gently stirring and tossing, until heated through, about 2 minutes. If the sauce appears too thick, add the reserved pasta water by the tablespoon (15 ml) while stirring, until it reaches the desired consistency

Plate and serve immediately.

SPAGHETTI WITH CLASSIC MARINARA

Many of the recipes in this book utilize packaged products like pasta sauce, chicken broth or ramen that we combine with fresh ingredients to make something quick and delicious. This is more of a made-from-scratch dish that takes some time but is totally worth the effort. You can really taste the difference between this marinara and the ones that you pour out of a jar. This sauce bursts with bright tomato flavor and the fresh basil really gives it a boost. A pinch of red pepper flakes provides a subtle kick, but you can omit it if you prefer. We love the simple, fresh taste of this sauce so much that we don't even add Parmesan cheese.

Serves 4

1 tbsp (15 ml) extra-virgin olive oil

1 medium yellow onion, chopped

4 garlic cloves, minced

½ tsp crushed red pepper flakes

1 tsp dried oregano

2 tbsp (36 g) plus 1 tsp kosher salt, divided

½ tsp black pepper

2 (28-oz [794-g]) cans whole peeled San Marzano tomatoes

10 fresh basil leaves, chopped

1 lb (454 g) dried spaghetti

Place a large skillet over medium-low heat and warm the olive oil. When the oil is hot, add the onion, garlic, red pepper flakes, oregano, 1 teaspoon of salt and pepper and cook, stirring occasionally, until the vegetables have softened, about 15 minutes. Add the tomatoes and their juices, increase the heat to medium and bring to a simmer. Reduce the heat to maintain a gentle simmer and cook, uncovered, for 1 hour. Occasionally stir and break up the tomatoes with a wooden spoon. Add the basil to the sauce, stir, cover and turn off the heat.

Meanwhile, to a large pot of water add 2 tablespoons (36 g) of salt and bring to a boil over high heat. Add the pasta and cook until al dente, stirring occasionally, according to the package directions. Drain the pasta and then transfer it to the skillet with the sauce or a large serving bowl, tossing to combine.

ORANGE CITRUS PESTO PASTA

With this recipe we wanted to create a fun play on pesto that really kicks up the bright, fresh citrus angle. The addition of a whole orange balances out the lemon juice, rounding out the flavors and preventing it from tasting too tart. By swapping out the customary pine nuts for almonds, this pesto also acquires pleasant nutty-sweet undertones. And finally, this version is completely vegan because it doesn't use Parmesan cheese. If you want, you can always grate some cheese to add as a last-minute garnish.

Serves 4

½ cup (12 g) fresh basil leaves

½ cup (54 g) slivered almonds

1 tsp chopped garlic

1 orange, peeled and roughly chopped (check for seeds and discard any)

Juice of ½ lemon

½ tsp kosher salt

½ tsp black pepper

¼ cup (60 ml) extra-virgin olive oil

10 oz (283 g) dried rotini

In a food processor or blender, place the basil, almonds, garlic, orange, lemon juice, salt and pepper and pulse until finely chopped, making sure to scrape down the sides a few times. With the machine running, slowly add the olive oil. Process until smooth, occasionally scraping down the sides, about 1 minute.

Bring a large pot of salted water to a boil over high heat. Add the pasta and cook until al dente, stirring occasionally, according to the package directions. Scoop out and reserve 1 cup (240 ml) of the pasta water before draining the pasta and returning it to the pot. Add the pesto and stir to combine. While stirring, slowly add the reserved pasta water a tablespoon (15 ml) at a time until you reach your desired consistency.

ASIAN—INSPIRED NOODLES

As we shared in the Introduction (page 7), our crazy journey toward Noodle Worship was set in motion by a single bowl of ramen. So it's not surprising that Asian noodles hold a very special place in our hearts. While we love all types of noodles, noodle soups, pastas and even pasta salads, we confess that many of our favorite recipes can be found in this chapter.

Our goal throughout this book—but in this chapter especially—was to remain as faithful as possible to the origins of classic dishes, while making the process accessible to the home cook. With some of the recipes in this chapter, you may need to make a trip to your nearest Asian market or shop online to get the authentic sauces and staple Asian ingredients. The little added effort, we can assure you, will be well worth the time. These days, however, it's getting easier and easier to track down many of these ingredients at your neighborhood grocery store.

Like many dishes in this book, we first discovered Spicy Peanut Noodles (page 53) not in a restaurant, but on social media. These noodles are very popular in New York, especially the ones served at Shu Jiao Fu Zhou restaurant on the Lower East Side. Judging by the reactions from people online, we knew we had to find a way to re-create the taste at home. We didn't have to travel far from home to try Garlicky Lo Mein with Shrimp (page 61), which is served all over Orange County. We've enjoyed this dish at a number of different spots, so the recipe that follows is a reflection and distillation of our favorite versions.

Don't forget to kick up these dishes with a healthy dose of your favorite chili oil like we do!

SPICY PEANUT NOODLES

We've been obsessed with knife-cut noodles ever since being introduced to them through social media. Maybe you've seen videos of chefs effortlessly slicing noodles off a big block of dough directly into a pot of boiling water. These famous Asian noodles are prized for their texture, which is chewy but soft. When shopping for them in markets or online, look for *dao xiao mian*, knife-cut noodles or knife-shaved noodles. Adding peanut butter to this noodle recipe results in a dish that is creamy, crispy, tangy and spicy. In this case, the chili crisp is not optional! If you want to dial up the heat even more, swap the regular sesame oil for sesame chili oil.

Serves 4

8 oz (226 g) knife-cut noodles or other wheat noodles

3 tbsp (48 g) smooth peanut butter

4 tsp (20 ml) rice vinegar

3 tsp (15 ml) soy sauce

4 tbsp (60 ml) chili crisp

2 tbsp (30 ml) sesame oil or sesame chili oil

2 tbsp (18 g) fried garlic, for garnish

4 scallions, thinly sliced, for garnish

Bring a large pot of water to a boil over high heat. Add the noodles and cook, stirring occasionally, according to the package directions. Scoop out and reserve 3 tablespoons (45 ml) of the cooking water before draining the noodles.

In a large mixing bowl, stir together the peanut butter, rice vinegar, soy sauce, chili crisp, sesame oil and 1 tablespoon (15 ml) of the reserved noodle water and mix until smooth. Add the cooked noodles and toss with tongs until they are completely coated in sauce. If the sauce appears too thick, add more reserved water by the tablespoon (15 ml), while stirring, until it reaches the desired consistency.

Divide the noodles among four bowls and top with the fried garlic and scallions.

GARLIC–CHILI NOODLES

This dish is all about the chili oil, that fire engine–red elixir that's a permanent fixture on the tables of every Sichuan restaurant. You could certainly buy a jar of it, but making it at home is surprisingly simple and the results are worth it. This chili oil is bold, fragrant and balanced— hot, but not blow-your-top hot. One of the best ways to enjoy freshly made Sichuan chili oil is, naturally, over noodles, in this case those great knife-cut wheat noodles from China. All it takes is some sliced scallions and cilantro (if you prefer) to complete the dish. If you find that you enjoy the chili oil as much as we do, consider making a double or triple batch to keep on hand; it lasts for weeks at room temperature and is great on everything from scrambled eggs to wontons.

Serves 2

1 scallion, thinly sliced

2 tbsp (18 g) minced garlic

4 tsp (20 ml) light soy sauce

2 tsp (10 ml) dark soy sauce

1 tsp black vinegar

2 tbsp (15 g) dried Sichuan red chili powder

½ tsp ground ginger

1 tsp kosher salt

8 oz (226 g) knife-cut noodles or other wheat noodles

6 tbsp (90 ml) vegetable oil

2 tbsp (2 g) chopped fresh cilantro, for garnish (optional)

In a medium mixing bowl, combine the scallion, garlic, light and dark soy sauces, black vinegar, chili powder, ginger and salt. Set aside.

Bring a large pot of water to a boil over high heat. Add the noodles and cook, stirring occasionally, according to the package directions. Drain and transfer them to a large mixing bowl when done.

Meanwhile, place a small saucepan over high heat and warm the vegetable oil. When the oil begins to smoke, carefully pour it into the bowl with the scallion mixture and whisk to combine. This is your chili oil! Add all of the chili oil to the noodles and toss or stir until thoroughly combined.

Plate and garnish with the cilantro (if using).

STIR-FRIED KIMCHI UDON

When we first discovered the joys of kimchi, we became obsessed and started trying to incorporate it into as many dishes as possible. The fermented vegetable dish brings fantastic crunch, heat and excitement to every bite. Here we pair it with thick, chewy udon, which creates a nice contrast in textures. The recipe also calls for kimchi juice, the liquid that is in the jar alongside the cabbage. You might have to go to an Asian foods market to track down a good-quality kimchi, but I think you'll agree that it's worth it.

Serves 4

SAUCE

2 tbsp (30 ml) kimchi juice

1 tsp sugar

1 tsp rice vinegar

1 tsp sesame chili oil

1 tsp black sesame seeds

1 tbsp (15 ml) soy sauce

NOODLES

14 oz (400 g) fresh udon

1 tbsp (15 ml) sesame oil

½ small yellow onion, sliced

1 cup (150 g) kimchi (any large pieces roughly chopped)

3 oz (85 g) sliced shitake mushrooms

2 scallions, thinly sliced, for garnish

1 tbsp (9 g) black sesame seeds, for garnish

To make the sauce, in a small mixing bowl, whisk together the kimchi juice, sugar, rice vinegar, sesame chili oil, sesame seeds and soy sauce until blended.

To make the noodles, bring a large pot of water to a boil over high heat. Add the noodles and cook, stirring occasionally, according to the package directions. Drain and set aside.

Place a wok or large skillet over medium-high heat and warm the sesame oil. When the oil is hot, add the onion and cook until translucent, about 2 minutes. Add the kimchi and mushrooms and cook until the mushrooms soften, about 3 minutes. Add the drained udon and the sauce and cook, while tossing or stirring, for 4 minutes.

Garnish with the scallions and black sesame seeds.

MARSEL'S GARLIC–PEPPER RAMEN

Over time, we have built up a pretty impressive pantry of Asian seasonings, which makes it easy to experiment in the kitchen. This recipe was made up on the fly using *nanami togarashi*, a slightly spicy, citrusy Japanese seasoning. The goal was to come up with a super-quick but flavorful recipe that used instant ramen without the included soup base. This recipe can be whipped up in about 5 minutes, making it ideal for a quick lunch. We named the dish after our two-year-old son Marsel, a notoriously picky eater who absolutely loves these noodles.

Serves 4

2 (3-oz [85-g]) packages ramen (we like Nongshim brand)

2 tsp (10 ml) sesame oil

2 garlic cloves, minced

¼ cup (60 ml) soy sauce

1½ tsp (3 g) nanami togarashi

2 scallions, thinly sliced, for garnish (optional)

1 tbsp (9 g) black sesame seeds, for garnish (optional)

Bring a large pot of water to a boil over high heat. Add the noodles and cook, stirring occasionally, according to the package directions. Drain the noodles and return them to the pot.

Meanwhile, place a medium saucepan over medium heat and warm the sesame oil. When the oil is hot, add the garlic and cook, while stirring, until lightly browned, about 45 seconds. Remove the saucepan from the heat, add the soy sauce and nanami togarashi and stir to blend. Add this mixture to the cooked noodles and stir to combine.

Divide the noodles among four bowls, and top with scallions (if using) and sesame seeds (if using).

GARLICKY LO MEIN WITH SHRIMP

This recipe is based on a traditional Asian dish, but we really kicked up the garlic flavors. By using heaps of freshly minced garlic along with some dried garlic powder, we achieve a much richer, fuller garlic profile. We think shrimp works so well in this recipe that we wouldn't even consider swapping it out for chicken, beef or pork. The results will be amazing whether you opt for the traditional style of leaving the tails on the shrimp or removing them. We also think that lo mein, made with eggs, provides the ideal texture and taste for this recipe, but feel free to use other noodles that you might have in the pantry. A drizzle of chili crisp takes this dish to the top!

Serves 4

10 oz (283 g) dried lo mein (egg noodles or spaghetti will work too)

3 tbsp (45 ml) soy sauce

1 tbsp (15 ml) oyster sauce

1 tbsp (8 g) garlic powder

1 tsp plus 1 tbsp (20 ml) sesame oil, divided

2 tbsp plus 1 tsp (21 g) minced garlic, divided

8 tbsp (112 g) unsalted butter, divided

2 scallions, thinly sliced, plus more for garnish

1 lb (454 g) medium tail-on shrimp, cleaned and deveined

Chili crisp, for garnish (optional)

Bring a large pot of water to a boil over high heat. Add the lo mein and cook, stirring occasionally, according to the package directions. Drain the noodles and set aside.

Meanwhile, in a medium bowl, combine the soy sauce, oyster sauce, garlic powder and 2 tablespoons (30 ml) of water.

Place a large skillet over medium heat. Put in 1 teaspoon of sesame oil and heat for 30 seconds. Add 2 tablespoons (18 g) of minced garlic and cook for 1 minute. Add 6 tablespoons (84 g) of butter and cook until the garlic begins to brown, about 1 minute. Add the soy sauce mixture and stir to combine. Reduce the heat to low, add the drained lo mein and the scallions and cook, stirring to combine, for 1 minute. Remove from the heat.

In a second large skillet over medium heat, place 1 tablespoon (15 ml) of sesame oil and heat for 30 seconds. Add 1 teaspoon of minced garlic and 2 tablespoons (28 g) of butter and stir to blend. Add the shrimp in a single layer and cook until they become opaque and the tails crisp up, 2 minutes per side. Transfer the cooked shrimp and any accumulated liquid to the skillet containing the noodles. Place the skillet over medium-low heat and cook for about 1 minute, stirring to combine and warm all the ingredients.

Divide the noodles and shrimp among four bowls, then garnish with scallions and chili crisp (if using).

SHANGHAI NOODLES

After tasting this famous Shanghainese pan-fried noodle dish in an Asian restaurant, we were absolutely obsessed. It stars fat, chewy udon that is tossed in a thick, dark and aromatic sauce. The key is Shaoxing cooking wine, which provides a subtle but distinctive sweet, nutty flavor. You can substitute cooking sherry if you can't track it down, but the dish will not taste nearly as amazing. Shanghai Noodles are typically made with pork, beef or no meat at all, but we decided to try it with chicken and were pleasantly surprised by how well it went with the marinade.

Serves 4

MARINADE

1 tsp Shaoxing wine

1 tsp light soy sauce

1 tsp dark soy sauce

1 tsp cornstarch

½ tsp sugar

8 oz (226 g) chicken breast, cut to 1-inch (2.5-cm) dice

UDON SAUCE

1 tsp Shaoxing wine

2½ tsp (12 ml) light soy sauce

2½ tsp (12 ml) dark soy sauce

1 tsp cornstarch

¼ tsp sugar

¼ tsp minced garlic

NOODLES

1 lb (454 g) fresh udon (we like Myojo brand)

1 bunch baby bok choy

1 tbsp (15 ml) sesame oil

8 scallions, cut into 2-inch (5-cm) pieces

To make the marinade, in a medium-sized mixing bowl, whisk the wine, light soy sauce, dark soy sauce, cornstarch and sugar until combined. Add the chicken breast and toss to coat. Cover and set aside to marinate at room temperature for 30 minutes.

To make the udon sauce, in a separate medium-sized mixing bowl, whisk the wine, light soy sauce, dark soy sauce, cornstarch, sugar and garlic until combined. Cover and set aside.

To make the noodles, bring a large pot of water to a boil over high heat. Add the udon and bok choy and cook for 2 minutes. Drain and separate the bok choy from the udon.

Place a wok or large skillet over medium heat and warm the sesame oil. When the oil is hot, add the chicken (discarding the marinade) and cook, while stirring, until lightly golden brown and nearly cooked through, about 5 minutes. Add the noodles and the udon sauce and cook, stirring constantly, for 2 minutes. Add the bok choy and scallions and cook, while stirring, for 2 minutes.

BANG BANG SHRIMP NOODLES

Bang bang shrimp is a favorite appetizer of ours, and whenever we see it on a restaurant menu, we're pretty much powerless to resist it. Typically, it consists of crispy fried shrimp in a sweet and savory sauce that gets its kick from Thai sweet chili sauce. We decided to turn that beloved appetizer into a main course by pairing it with pasta. Because of that, we chose not to batter and fry the shrimp, but instead season and sauté it to keep it on the lighter side. The result is a noodle dish that has the same great flavors—if not necessarily the textures—of the original bang bang shrimp.

Serves 4

SAUCE

½ cup (120 ml) plain unsweetened Greek yogurt

1½ tsp (7 ml) sriracha

1½ tsp (4 g) minced garlic

⅓ cup (80 ml) sweet Thai chili sauce

Juice of ½ a lime

NOODLES

8 oz (226 g) dried spaghetti

10 oz (283 g) shrimp, peeled and deveined

Pinch of sweet paprika

Pinch of kosher salt

Pinch of black pepper

2 tbsp (28 g) butter

2 tsp (6 g) minced garlic

1 tbsp (4 g) chopped fresh parsley, for garnish

⅛ tsp crushed red pepper flakes, for garnish (optional)

In a medium bowl, whisk the yogurt, sriracha, garlic, chili sauce and lime juice until well combined. Set aside.

Bring a large pot of salted water to a boil over high heat. Add the pasta and cook until al dente, stirring occasionally, according to the package directions. Drain and set aside.

Meanwhile, in a large bowl, combine the shrimp, paprika, salt and pepper and toss to coat. Place a large skillet over medium-high heat and warm the butter. When the butter has melted, add the shrimp, arranged in a single layer, and cook for 90 seconds. Flip the shrimp and continue cooking for 90 seconds. Add the garlic and cook, stirring constantly, for 30 seconds. Remove the shrimp from the heat, add the yogurt–chili sauce mixture and drained pasta and toss or stir with tongs until everything is well combined.

Plate and garnish with parsley and red pepper flakes (if using).

FIERY RAM-DON

Ram-don is the dish made famous by the South Korean film *Parasite*. The name comes from the two instant noodle types that are used in the recipe: ramen and udon. Of course, Korean food fans might know the dish by its traditional name, *jjapaguri*. In that popular movie, the typically budget-friendly instant noodle bowl is topped with high-quality beef, which really elevates the experience. We do the same here, but we also kick things up by adding some sesame chili oil, which is why we call this dish "fiery." If you want to eliminate the spice, you can swap in regular sesame oil instead.

Serves 4

12 oz (340 g) sirloin or ribeye steak, cut to ³⁄₄-inch (2-cm) dice

½ tbsp (6 g) kosher salt

2½ tbsp (38 ml) ponzu sauce

2 tsp (10 ml) vegetable oil

2 (4.5-oz [127-g]) packages chapagetti

2 (4.2-oz [120-g]) packages neoguri

2 scallions, thinly sliced, for garnish

Sesame chili oil or regular sesame oil to taste, for garnish

In a medium bowl, stir together the steak, salt and ponzu sauce. Cover the bowl and set aside to marinate for 30 minutes.

Place a large skillet over medium-high heat and warm the vegetable oil. When the oil is hot, add the steak (discarding the marinade) in a single layer. Cook, without stirring, until golden brown, about 2 minutes. Flip the steak and continue cooking until medium, about 2 minutes. Transfer to a plate, cover and set aside.

Bring a large pot of water to a boil over high heat. Add all four packages of instant noodles (setting aside all of the seasoning packets for now) and cook, stirring occasionally, for 3 minutes. Scoop out and reserve 2 cups (480 ml) of the noodle water. Drain, but do not rinse, the noodles.

In a large bowl, combine the reserved noodle water and the contents of all of the seasoning packets that came with the four packages of noodles, including any soup bases, vegetables and/or oil. The exact contents of the seasonings may vary from brand to brand; that's okay, just add them all. Whisk together. Add the drained noodles and toss until the noodles are completely coated with the sauce. Add the steak and toss to combine.

Divide among four bowls, and top with the scallions and sesame chili oil.

DAN DAN NOODLES

The first time we experienced dan dan noodles was at Z & Y Restaurant, the famous Sichuan destination in San Francisco. We love noodles (obviously!) and we are always on the hunt for the best, which brought us to that Michelin-ranked hot spot. After one bite, we were immediately hooked. This is a layered noodle dish with an amazing array of textures and flavors. After the noodles are cooked and tossed in the nutty sesame sauce, they are topped with the various garnishes, which are stirred into the noodles at the table. Our favorite part is the crispy pork. For recipes like this one that have a lot of ingredients, some of which are not always easy to find, we endeavor to strip it down to the essentials. We think that this wonderful recipe is the perfect compromise between authentic flavor and minimal effort.

Serves 4–6

TAHINI SAUCE

⅓ cup (80 ml) tahini

3 garlic cloves, minced

1 tbsp (5 g) grated ginger

2 tbsp (30 ml) chili oil with sesame seeds

1 tbsp (15 ml) sesame oil

1 tbsp (15 ml) black vinegar

2 tbsp (30 ml) soy sauce

1 tsp sugar

PORK

1 tbsp (15 ml) vegetable oil

12 oz (340 g) ground pork

1 tbsp (15 ml) black vinegar

1 tbsp (15 ml) hoisin sauce

2 tsp (10 ml) soy sauce

NOODLES

1 lb (454 g) dan dan or thin wheat noodles

2 tbsp (16 g) chopped roasted peanuts, for garnish

2 scallions, thinly sliced, for garnish

½ cup (120 ml) chili oil with sesame seeds, for garnish

To make the tahini sauce, in a medium bowl, whisk the tahini, garlic, ginger, chili oil, sesame oil, black vinegar, soy sauce and sugar until blended. Set aside.

To make the pork, place a large skillet over medium-high heat and warm the vegetable oil. Add the ground pork and cook, breaking the meat apart with a wooden spoon, until lightly browned, about 8 minutes. Add the black vinegar, hoisin sauce and soy sauce and cook, stirring occasionally, until the liquid has evaporated, about 5 minutes. Remove from the heat and keep warm until ready to serve.

Meanwhile, make the noodles. Bring a large pot of water to a boil over high heat. Add the noodles and cook, stirring occasionally, according to the package directions. Drain the noodles, add them to the tahini sauce and stir until completely coated.

Divide the noodles among bowls, top with the pork, peanuts and scallions, then drizzle with the chili oil.

GARLIC–BUTTER SHRIMP RAMEN

Of all the noodles in the world, ramen is our absolute favorite. For a couple of years, we were enjoying ramen as a family four to five times per week. We know that we're not alone in our obsession with ramen. It's incredibly popular because it's affordable, it's quick and easy to make, it's filling and flavorful, and it's fun to get creative with modifications and add-ons. Over the years, we've experimented with all sorts of tricks and techniques that take packaged ramen to the next level. A few fresh ingredients are all you need to transform that boring "cup o' noodles" into restaurant-quality ramen. Some packaged ramen brands call for adding the soup base to the boiling water, but others (like the ones we use here) instruct that it be added to the bowl of cooked noodles. Just follow the instructions for the type you are using.

Serves 4

16 medium shrimp, peeled and deveined

2 tsp (12 g) kosher salt

1 tsp crushed red pepper flakes

½ tsp sweet paprika

4 tbsp (56 g) unsalted butter

4 tsp (11 g) minced garlic

4 (5.5-oz [155-g]) packages garlic or regular miso ramen with soup base

TOPPING

4 garlic cloves, pressed or minced

4 scallions, thinly sliced

4 tsp (12 g) black sesame seeds

Place a large pot of salted water over high heat and bring to a boil.

Meanwhile, pat the shrimp dry with paper towels and place them in a large bowl. Add the salt, red pepper flakes and paprika and toss to combine.

Place a large skillet over medium-high heat and warm the butter. When the butter begins to foam, add the shrimp in a single layer and cook for 2 minutes per side. Add the garlic and continue cooking for about 2 minutes, or until the shrimp turn opaque and the garlic is fragrant, being careful not to burn the garlic.

When the water comes to a boil, add the ramen and cook, according to the package directions.

Place one packet of soup base into each of four bowls. Drain the ramen and divide the noodles evenly among the bowls. Toss to combine with the soup base. Top each bowl with four shrimp and the garlic, scallions and black sesame seeds.

GREEN ONION OIL NOODLES

This unique Asian dish is so quick and simple to make, yet so packed with flavor and texture that it has become one of our favorite things to make at home. Most of the flavor comes from the oil, which gets infused with savory onion flavor from the scallions. The trickiest part is getting the heat just right so that the green onions give off their flavor without burning. You really want to push them right up to the line between lightly charred and burnt, stopping short of the latter. In addition to the wonderful flavor they give to the oil, the scallions add a crispy texture to the final dish.

Serves 4

12 oz (340 g) thin wheat noodles

4 tbsp (60 ml) vegetable oil

6 scallions, 4 cut to 2-inch (5-cm) lengths and 2 thinly sliced, divided

2 tbsp (30 ml) light soy sauce

2 tbsp (30 ml) dark soy sauce

1 tsp sugar

Bring a large pot of water to a boil over high heat. Add the noodles and cook, stirring occasionally, according to the package directions. Drain, rinse with cold water and drain again.

Place a wok or large skillet over medium-low heat and warm the vegetable oil. When the oil is hot, add the 2-inch (5-cm) scallions. Cook, while tossing or stirring, until golden brown, about 5 minutes. Immediately remove the scallions from the wok, place them on a paper towel–lined plate to drain and set aside.

In the wok, cook the light and dark soy sauces and the sugar until the mixture starts to bubble. Remove from the heat and add the noodles. Toss or stir the noodles until they are fully coated in the sauce. Depending on the temperature of the wok and sauce, you might want to heat the noodles over low heat for a couple of minutes to warm through.

Divide the noodles among four bowls, then top with the crispy scallions and sliced fresh scallions.

SHRIMP PAD THAI

Like most families, we love ordering pad thai from the neighborhood Thai restaurant. But as seafood lovers, we often feel a little bit cheated on the number of shrimp that come in each portion. For the same amount of money (and not much more time), we discovered that we could prepare it at home with double the amount of seafood. That alone makes it more than worth the added effort. For this version, we use jarred pad thai sauce, which really speeds up the cooking process without sacrificing those classic flavors. Rice noodles, sometimes sold as pad thai noodles, just need a quick soak in warm water before going into the wok or skillet.

Serves 4–6

12 oz (340 g) ¼-inch (6-mm)-wide rice noodles

2½ tbsp (37 ml) vegetable oil

12 oz (340 g) large shrimp, shelled and deveined

3 garlic cloves, minced

2 eggs

1 cup (240 ml) pad thai sauce

2 cups (208 g) bean sprouts

1 cup (48 g) chives, cut into 2-inch (5-cm) pieces

TOPPING

2 tbsp (18 g) chopped peanuts

1 lime, cut into wedges

Sriracha (optional)

Soak the rice noodles in warm water until soft, about 10 minutes.

Place a wok or large skillet over medium-high heat and warm the vegetable oil. When the oil is hot, add the shrimp and garlic. Cook the shrimp for 90 seconds per side. Add the noodles and cook, while tossing or stirring, for 1 minute. Once the shrimp turn opaque, slide the shrimp and noodles to one side of the wok. In the open space, cook the eggs, stirring until scrambled, about 3 minutes. Mix the eggs into the noodles and toss or stir to combine everything evenly for 1 minute. Add the pad thai sauce and toss or stir to completely coat the noodles. Reduce the heat to low, add the bean sprouts and chives and cook, while tossing or stirring, for 1 minute.

Remove the wok from the heat, divide among bowls and top the noodles with the peanuts and lime wedges, and Sriracha to taste (if using).

SPICY SOY SAUCE CHOW MEIN

One of our favorite Chinese takeout meals is chow mein. And one of our favorite ways to enjoy it is with *just a little too much* Chinese hot mustard. We wanted to see if we could come up with a recipe that satisfied our cravings for the restaurant dish, but was quick and easy and relied on ingredients that we typically have on hand. This recipe checks all the boxes. Although it takes almost no time to prepare, the finished dish is loaded with umami goodness and just enough heat and sweetness to satisfy those feel-good food cravings. If you want to experience the dish like we do, go ahead and pile on the hot mustard!

Serves 2–4

8 oz (226 g) dried chow mein (see Note)

6 tbsp (90 ml) dark soy sauce

4 tsp (20 ml) light soy sauce

½ cup (120 ml) black vinegar

4 tsp (16 g) sugar

2 tbsp (30 ml) sesame chili oil

4 tsp (20 ml) chili crisp

2 tbsp (30 ml) sesame oil

2 scallions, thinly sliced, for garnish

Chinese hot mustard, for garnish (optional)

Bring a large pot of water to a boil over high heat. Add the noodles and cook, stirring occasionally, according to the package directions. Drain, rinse with cold water and drain again.

In a medium bowl, whisk the dark soy sauce, light soy sauce, black vinegar, sugar, sesame chili oil and chili crisp until combined. Set aside.

Place a wok or large skillet over high heat and warm the sesame oil. When the oil begins to smoke, add the noodles and cook, without stirring, until crispy, about 2 minutes. Flip the noodles and continue cooking, without stirring, for 2 minutes. Add the soy sauce mixture and cook, while stirring or tossing, for 90 seconds.

Divide the noodles among bowls and top with the scallions and hot mustard (if using).

Note: When shopping for the noodles, make sure to get chow mein of the stir-fry variety, not the crunchy condiment kind.

AMERICAN, SOUTHERN & SOUTHWESTERN COMFORT FOOD

When we think of comfort food, our minds invariably wander to regions like the American South, Southwest and Deep South. In places like these, cooks really seem to know how to make family and friends feel good by cooking from the heart.

Depending on one's background, comfort food will mean different things to different people. But to us, the thing that unites these recipes is an underlying feeling of gratification. How can a person not feel the (figurative) embrace of a warm hug when digging into a big bowl of Buttery Egg Noodles with Pull-Apart Cheesy Garlic Bread (page 93)? Some dishes, like the undeniably over-the-top Easy Fried Chicken Mac 'n' Cheese (page 81), manage to pack two legendary comfort foods into one epic meal. And of course, it wouldn't be Noodle Worship without a few tasty twists. As the name implies, Taco Pasta (page 89) transforms all the best qualities of tacos into a savory, delicious pasta dish. In that fun recipe, we swap one shell (tortilla) for another (pasta).

Just because the recipes in the following chapter happen to be immensely fulfilling, it doesn't mean they are time intensive. Dishes like the luscious Avocado Penne (page 90) can be whipped up in no time after a long day of work, providing the whole family with a much-needed dose of sustenance and good cheer.

EASY FRIED CHICKEN MAC 'N' CHEESE

No offense to peanut butter and jelly, but there might be no better food combination than fried chicken and macaroni and cheese. The textural interplay between the crispy, batter-fried chicken and the silky-soft goodness of the mac and cheese is the yin and yang we crave. While mac and cheese is a common side dish to fried chicken, we plate the pair together to make things easy. And to make the frying part less stressful, we ditch the traditional large pieces of chicken in favor of bite-size pieces of dark meat, which we toss in a pre-seasoned chicken batter mix and cook in a regular skillet instead of a deep-fryer.

Serves 4

10 oz (283 g) dried elbow macaroni

3 tbsp (42 g) butter

1 (12-oz [354-ml]) can evaporated milk

¾ cup (85 g) shredded pepper Jack cheese

¾ cup (85 g) shredded sharp cheddar cheese

1 (9-oz [255-g]) bag seasoned chicken batter mix, divided (we like Louisiana Fish Fry Products)

3 skinless, boneless chicken thighs, cut into 1-inch (2.5-cm) cubes

1 cup (240 ml) vegetable oil

Bring a large pot of salted water to a boil over high heat. Add the macaroni and cook until al dente, stirring occasionally, according to the package directions. Drain the pasta and return the macaroni to the pot. Add the butter and stir until the butter has melted and the pasta is fully coated.

Meanwhile, place a large saucepan over medium-high heat, and bring the evaporated milk to a boil. Reduce the heat to low, add the pepper Jack and cheddar cheeses and whisk until completely melted and smooth, about 5 minutes. Carefully add the buttered macaroni and cook, while stirring, for 4 minutes. Keep warm over very low heat while you cook the chicken.

In a large mixing bowl, whisk 5 tablespoons (40 g) of the chicken batter mix and ½ cup (120 ml) of cold water until well combined. Place the remaining batter mix in a separate shallow bowl. Working with a few pieces at a time, dip the chicken in the liquid batter, allowing the excess to drip off, then dredge the chicken in the dry batter mix to evenly coat it. Repeat this process with the remaining chicken.

Place a large skillet over medium-high heat. Pour in the oil and heat to 350°F (175°C). Working in batches, fry the chicken until golden brown, crispy and cooked through, about 2 minutes per side. Transfer to a paper towel–lined plate to drain while you fry the rest.

Divide the macaroni and cheese among four bowls and top with the fried chicken bites.

CREOLE SHRIMP & SAUSAGE ALFREDO

Throughout this cookbook, we have not been shy about taking shortcuts when the ends justify the means. That approach definitely applies here, where we proudly lean on Tony Chachere's Original Creole Seasoning to provide the authentic flavors of the Big Easy. We find that this particular blend of herbs and spices melds perfectly with shrimp. But for this recipe to truly achieve greatness you *must* use andouille sausage—this heavily spiced, smoked pork sausage is a staple in Creole and Cajun cooking. We bring the dish home with a lush, velvety sauce that fills the penne pasta tubes with little drops of love.

Serves 4–6

10 oz (283 g) shrimp, peeled and deveined

1½ tbsp (10 g) Creole or Cajun seasoning (we like Tony Chachere's)

2 tbsp (28 g) butter

10 oz (283 g) sliced andouille sausage

1 medium yellow onion, diced

3 garlic cloves, minced

10 oz (283 g) dried penne

¼ cup (60 ml) chicken broth

2 cups (480 ml) heavy cream

1 cup (100 g) freshly grated Parmesan cheese

Kosher salt and black pepper to taste

In a large bowl, combine the shrimp and Creole seasoning and toss to coat.

Place a large skillet over medium heat and warm the butter. When the butter has melted, add the shrimp, arranged in a single layer, and cook for 2 minutes. Flip and continue cooking for 2 minutes. Transfer the shrimp to a plate.

In the same skillet over medium heat, cook the sausage and onion until the sausage is lightly browned and the onion softens, about 6 minutes. Add the garlic and cook for 1 minute. Transfer the sausage and onion to the plate with the shrimp.

Bring a large pot of salted water to a boil over high heat. Add the pasta and cook until al dente, stirring occasionally, according to the package directions.

Meanwhile, to the same skillet over medium heat, add the chicken broth, scraping up any browned bits in the pan with a wooden spoon, until the broth reduces by half, about 5 minutes. Reduce the heat to medium-low and add the cream. When the sauce comes to a gentle simmer, add the Parmesan and cook, while stirring, until fully incorporated and smooth, about 3 minutes. Season to taste with salt and pepper. Add the shrimp, sausage and onion and stir to blend. Add the drained pasta and stir well to combine.

CAJUN LIME SHRIMP PASTA

Once we became acquainted with Cajun seasoning mix, we began looking for new and interesting ways to utilize it in the kitchen. We would characterize it as being more zesty than spicy, and the distinctive combination of spices introduces a warm, earthy, savory flavor component to recipes like this one. Since seafood is king in Cajun country, we decided to add shrimp, which gets a quick marinade in the seasonings. The resulting dish is along the lines of a creamy alfredo sauce with a slight kick. The addition of lime juice at the end really cuts through some of the richness in the dish. We suggest adding the juice a little bit at a time until you find your own sweet spot.

Serves 4

12 oz (340 g) dried linguine

1 lb (454 g) shrimp, cleaned and deveined

1 tbsp (15 ml) extra-virgin olive oil

2 tbsp (12 g) Cajun seasoning

1 tbsp (14 g) unsalted butter

1 cup (240 ml) heavy cream

½ cup (50 g) grated Parmesan cheese

Juice of 1½ small limes, or more to taste

Kosher salt (optional)

Black pepper (optional)

Bring a large pot of salted water to a boil over high heat. Add the pasta and cook until al dente, stirring occasionally, according to the package directions. Scoop out and reserve ½ cup (120 ml) of the pasta water before draining the pasta.

Meanwhile, in a large mixing bowl, toss together the shrimp, olive oil and Cajun seasoning.

Place a large skillet over medium-high heat and warm the butter. When the butter has melted, add the shrimp in a single layer and cook for 2 minutes per side. Transfer the shrimp to a plate, but leave any accumulated juices in the skillet.

Reduce the heat to medium, add the cream and stir with a wooden spoon to scrape up any bits on the bottom of the skillet. Reduce the heat to low, then add the Parmesan and stir until melted and the sauce is smooth. Add the lime juice and stir to combine. Taste and adjust the seasoning, adding salt, pepper or additional lime juice, if desired.

Add the shrimp and drained pasta to the sauce and stir to blend. If the sauce appears too thick, add the reserved pasta water by the tablespoon (15 ml), while stirring, until it reaches the desired consistency.

Plate and serve immediately.

FOUR–CHEESE BROCCOLI PAPPARDELLE

Broccoli with cheese sauce is a time-tested food that encourages the little ones to eat their veggies. We decided to upgrade the classic dish in a few ways that we believe makes it more elegant and delicious. The first is with the addition of pappardelle pasta, which transforms the tasty side dish into a satisfying main course. We also boost the typically one-dimensional cheddar cheese sauce by using a four-cheese blend that adds some depth of flavor. Each of the four cheeses brings something unique to the table and, when combined, the results are out of this world. We don't always use real, imported Parmigiano-Reggiano when cooking because it is more expensive than generic Parmesan, but it really does make a huge difference—especially when freshly grated. We suggest you give it a try and judge for yourself.

Serves 4–6

1 lb (454 g) dried pappardelle

1¼ cups (300 ml) whole milk

¾ cup (75 g) grated Asiago cheese

¾ cup (75 g) grated fontina cheese

⅛ tsp black pepper

¾ cup (75 g) grated Pecorino Romano cheese

¾ cup (75 g) grated Parmigiano-Reggiano cheese

Kosher salt to taste

2 cups (182 g) frozen broccoli florets, thawed (see Note)

Bring a large pot of salted water to a boil over high heat. Add the pasta and cook until al dente, stirring occasionally, according to the package directions.

Meanwhile, place a large saucepan over medium heat, pour in the milk and bring to a simmer. Reduce the heat to low, add the Asiago and fontina, and whisk until completely melted and smooth, about 5 minutes. Whisk in the black pepper. Add the pecorino and Parmigiano-Reggiano and whisk until completely melted and smooth, about 5 minutes. Remove from the heat and season to taste with salt.

When the pasta is done, transfer it with tongs directly from the water to the saucepan. Add the broccoli and stir until everything is fully coated with sauce.

Plate and serve immediately.

Note: We used frozen broccoli to keep things easy, but fresh broccoli would be great if you have it on hand. Add it to the boiling water with the pasta during the last 2 minutes of the pasta's cook time. Drain the broccoli and pasta together and add it to the saucepan with the sauce.

TACO PASTA

If your family is at all like ours, you likely have fond memories of sitting around the dinner table to enjoy homestyle foods like Hamburger Helper™ and chili mac. Dishes like those relied on pasta, canned tomatoes and spices to stretch a little ground beef into a delicious family-sized meal. This recipe is designed to evoke those feelings of nostalgia, while upping the fresh-flavor factor. As the name suggests, this dish transforms the wonderful flavor of tacos into a savory pasta. By cooking the pasta in the same pan as the meat sauce, it absorbs all of that great flavor while reducing the number of dishes to clean—a win-win.

Serves 4

8 oz (226 g) ground beef (80/20)

½ white onion, diced

1 garlic clove, minced

2 cups (480 ml) chicken stock

2 tbsp (6 g) taco seasoning

½ cup (120 ml) red taco sauce

½ cup (120 ml) tomato sauce

6 oz (170 g) dried medium pasta shells

¼ cup (60 ml) heavy cream

2 cups (226 g) grated sharp cheddar cheese

½ tomato, chopped

2 tbsp (2 g) chopped fresh cilantro, for garnish

Place a large saucepan or Dutch oven over medium heat. Cook the ground beef, breaking the meat apart with a wooden spoon, until lightly browned, about 5 minutes. Add the onion and garlic and cook, stirring occasionally, until the vegetables are softened, about 2 minutes.

Add the chicken stock, taco seasoning, taco sauce and tomato sauce and stir to combine. Increase the heat to high and add the uncooked pasta. When the sauce comes to a simmer, reduce the heat to low and cook, covered, until the pasta is al dente, about 12 minutes.

Remove from the heat and stir in the cream. Working with roughly a handful at a time, add the cheddar and stir until completely melted and smooth.

Top with the tomato and cilantro.

AVOCADO PENNE

We'll admit that avocado sauce on pasta might sound a bit out of left field, but give it a chance—especially if you love avocados like we do. This is a very quick, simple sauce that doesn't even need to be cooked, rather just warmed from the cooked pasta. This technique preserves the fresh, mild and buttery flavor of avocados. Fresh-squeezed lemon juice is essential in this dish, but the red pepper flakes are not. If you don't like spice, feel free to leave them out.

Serves 4–6

12 oz (340 g) dried penne

1 large avocado, halved, peeled and pitted

2 tbsp (30 ml) lemon juice

¼ cup (60 ml) extra-virgin olive oil

1 tsp minced garlic

Kosher salt and black pepper to taste

2 scallions, thinly sliced, for garnish

Pinch of crushed red pepper flakes, for garnish (optional)

Bring a large pot of salted water to a boil over high heat. Add the pasta and cook until al dente, stirring occasionally, according to the package directions. Scoop out and reserve ½ cup (120 ml) of the pasta water before draining the pasta.

In a food processor or blender, combine the avocado, lemon juice, olive oil and garlic and process until smooth, making sure to scrape down the sides a few times. Add the reserved pasta water and pulse to blend. Season to taste with salt and pepper.

Return the pasta to the pot (making sure the heat is off), add the avocado sauce and stir to blend.

Plate and garnish with the scallions and red pepper flakes (if using).

BUTTERY EGG NOODLES WITH PULL–APART CHEESY GARLIC BREAD

There is nothing more comforting than a big bowl of buttered noodles. We've improved upon this classic kid-friendly dish by going with wide egg noodles, which manage to make it even more satisfying. But what takes it to the next level is the nutty toasted garlic and fresh parsley. We decided to level up the comfort factor by pairing this delectable dish with a fun-to-eat, pull-apart cheesy garlic bread. All we can say is, proceed with caution, because you might find it very difficult to step away from the table!

Serves 4

PULL-APART CHEESY GARLIC BREAD

1 (1-lb [454-g]) loaf French bread

8 tbsp (112 g) salted butter

3 garlic cloves, minced

2 tbsp (8 g) chopped fresh parsley, divided

1 cup (112 g) shredded mozzarella cheese

BUTTERY EGG NOODLES

2 tbsp (36 g) kosher salt, plus more as needed

8 oz (226 g) dried wide egg noodles

¼ cup (57 g) salted butter

2 tsp (6 g) minced garlic

1 tbsp (4 g) chopped fresh parsley

½ cup (50 g) freshly grated Parmesan cheese

Black pepper to taste

Preheat the oven to 375°F (190°C).

To make the cheesy garlic bread, use a serrated knife to score the loaf lengthwise and then crosswise to create a 1-inch (2.5-cm)-wide grid pattern. Be careful to not slice all the way through the loaf.

Place a small saucepan over medium-low heat and warm the butter. When the butter has melted, add the garlic and 1 tablespoon (4 g) of parsley and stir to blend. Remove from the heat. Using a pastry brush, evenly apply the butter mixture to the entire surface of the bread as well as inside all of the cracks and crevices. Then evenly distribute the cheese inside all the crevices.

Place the bread on a sheet pan, cover it with aluminum foil and cook for 30 minutes. Remove the foil and continue cooking until the cheese is fully melted, about 15 minutes. Remove the bread from the oven and garnish it with the remaining 1 tablespoon (4 g) of parsley.

While the bread is baking, make the buttery egg noodles. Bring a large pot of water with 2 tablespoons (36 g) of salt to a boil over high heat. Add the noodles and cook until al dente, stirring occasionally, according to package directions. Scoop out and reserve ½ cup (120 ml) of the noodle water before draining the noodles.

Meanwhile, place a large skillet over medium heat and warm the butter. When the butter begins to bubble, add the garlic and cook, stirring constantly, until lightly golden brown, about 2 minutes. Remove the pan from the heat.

Add the noodles to the skillet and stir to combine. Stir in the reserved noodle water by the tablespoon (15 ml) until you achieve a silky, creamy consistency. Stir in the parsley followed by the Parmesan. Season to taste with salt and pepper and serve with the garlic bread.

DELECTABLE OVEN–BAKED PASTA

If you're on the hunt for family-style comfort food that can feed a crowd, then this is the chapter for you. Whenever we feel like stepping up our nest-and-chill factor, we instinctively gravitate towards a baked pasta casserole like the ones that follow. There's nothing more enjoyable than gathering at the dinner table around a big, bubbly, beautiful crock of baked noodles, sauce and cheese. We normally don't even bother with slicing and serving, instead just letting each person scoop away as desired.

The recipes in this chapter often have more ingredients and steps—including some ever-so-slightly-complicated techniques—than elsewhere in the book, but if we can do it, then you definitely can too. The good news is that all the work is front-loaded, meaning that when the dish goes into the oven, your work is done!

Of course, the big payoff comes when you spoon out heaping portions of tender noodles, melty cheese and savory meat sauce like those in the Cheesy Baked Mostaccioli (page 106), a sort of free-form lasagna. If you've never tasted a baked pasta dish starring tender gnocchi, turn to pages 97 and 102 and prepare to be blown away. For a dish that will fulfill your dreams, try a fragrant plate of Greek Pastitsio (page 110), a Greek-style lasagna with a cinnamon-scented béchamel sauce.

Don't be intimidated; you got this!

BAKED GNOCCHI WITH SAUSAGE & KALE

When you have children like we do, you're always looking for ways to sneak some healthy veggies into their meals. One of the easiest ways to do that, we have found, is to incorporate them into cheesy baked casseroles like this one. Four cups of kale might look and sound like a ton of greens, but they cook down considerably. And when tucked into a fontina-based cheese sauce, who's going to complain? We think the pairing of sausage and kale is unbeatable, and if you've never made a baked pasta dish with gnocchi, you have no idea how delicious dinner can be.

Serves 6

1 lb (454 g) gnocchi

4 cups (268 g) roughly chopped kale (stems removed)

1 lb (454 g) ground Italian sausage

2 tbsp (28 g) butter

½ white onion, finely chopped

3 garlic cloves, minced

2 tbsp (16 g) all-purpose flour

1½ cups (360 ml) whole milk

¾ cup (84 g) shredded fontina cheese

Zest of 1 lemon

Kosher salt and black pepper to taste

½ cup (50 g) grated Parmesan cheese

Preheat the oven to 400°F (200°C). Grease a 9 x 13-inch (23 x 33-cm) baking dish with nonstick cooking spray and set aside.

Bring a large pot of salted water to a boil over high heat. Add the pasta and cook until al dente, stirring occasionally, according to the package directions. When there is 1 minute remaining in the cook time, add the kale. Drain the gnocchi and kale and return them to the pot.

Meanwhile, place a medium skillet over medium-high heat. Cook the sausage, breaking the meat apart with a wooden spoon, until nicely browned, about 8 minutes. Transfer to a paper towel-lined plate to drain.

Reduce the heat to medium and cook the butter and onion until the onion begins to soften, about 4 minutes. Add the garlic and cook for 30 seconds. Add the flour and stir to combine. While whisking, slowly add the milk. Cook, whisking steadily, until the sauce has thickened, about 3 minutes. Add the fontina and lemon zest and stir until completely melted and smooth, about 3 minutes. Season with the salt and pepper to taste.

Add the cooked sausage and cheese sauce to the gnocchi and kale and stir to combine. Transfer this mixture to the baking dish, top with Parmesan cheese and cook, uncovered, until lightly golden brown and bubbly, about 20 minutes.

SPICY SAUSAGE LASAGNA

Our family adores lasagna, one of those classic comfort foods that never seem to go out of fashion. Larone's mother makes some fantastic Italian dishes, and she has been making versions of this recipe forever. We like spicy foods in our family, so naturally she substituted the typical ground beef for spicy Italian sausage and added some red pepper flakes. In another time-saving move, we use jarred marinara instead of cooked-from-scratch sauce and have gotten zero complaints from eaters. Use a spicy marinara (Rao's Homemade® has a great one, if you can find it) in conjunction with the spicy sausage and pepper flakes to take the heat to diablo level! If you prefer less spice, you can always use mild sausage and use just a pinch of, or even omit, the pepper flakes.

Serves 8

9 lasagna sheets

1 lb (454 g) ricotta cheese

1½ tbsp (6 g) chopped fresh flat-leaf parsley

1 egg

1 tbsp (15 ml) extra-virgin olive oil

1 medium yellow onion, chopped

1 lb (454 g) ground hot Italian sausage

4 garlic cloves, minced

¼ tsp red pepper flakes

2 (24-oz [642-ml]) jars marinara (we like Rao's Homemade brand, either regular or spicy)

Kosher salt and black pepper to taste

4 cups (448 g) shredded mozzarella cheese

¾ cup (75 g) grated Parmesan cheese

1 tbsp (4 g) chopped fresh basil, for garnish

Preheat the oven to 375°F (190°C). Grease a 9 x 13-inch (23 x 33-cm) baking dish with either cooking spray or olive oil.

Bring a large pot of salted water to a boil over high heat. Add the pasta and cook until al dente, stirring occasionally, according to the package directions. Drain, rinse with cold water and drain again. Arrange the noodles on a sheet pan to keep them from sticking together.

Meanwhile, in a medium mixing bowl, combine the ricotta, parsley and egg and stir to blend. Refrigerate until needed.

Place a large saucepan over medium heat and pour in the olive oil. When the oil is hot, add the onion and cook, stirring occasionally, until the onion begins to soften, about 4 minutes. Add the sausage and cook, breaking the meat apart with a wooden spoon, until nicely browned, about 8 minutes. Add the garlic and red pepper flakes and cook for 30 seconds. Reduce the heat to low, add the marinara and cook, stirring occasionally, for 15 minutes. Season to taste with salt and pepper.

In the greased baking dish, add 1 cup (240 ml) of the sauce and spread it out in an even layer. Arrange 3 cooked noodles lengthwise over the sauce. Top with one-third of the remaining sauce. Dollop on half of the ricotta and egg mixture. Evenly distribute one-third of the mozzarella and one-third of the Parmesan. Arrange 3 more noodles on top, followed by half of the remaining sauce, all of the remaining ricotta mixture, half of the remaining mozzarella and half of the remaining Parmesan. Arrange the last 3 noodles on top, followed by the rest of the sauce and the remaining mozzarella and Parmesan.

Spray the underside of a piece of aluminum foil before covering the baking dish and bake for 35 minutes. Remove the foil and continue baking until golden brown and bubbly, about 15 minutes. Garnish with the basil and let it cool for 15 minutes before slicing and serving.

NENE'S MAC 'N' CHEESE

If you're a mac and cheese lover like we are, you're going to want to make this dish. It is based on Larone's mom's recipe, but with a few tweaks. The addition of nutty, aromatic Gruyère definitely elevates this dish to grown-up status, while the sharp cheddar and dash of cayenne add some bite. Many home cooks make their mac and cheese on a stovetop, but we prefer to go a step further and bake it. Nothing compares to that golden brown and bubbly crust, which is how our family has always enjoyed it.

Serves 8–10

1 lb (454 g) elbow macaroni

¾ cup (170 g) unsalted butter, divided

⅓ cup (41 g) all-purpose flour

2½ cups (600 ml) whole milk

1½ cups (360 ml) heavy whipping cream

4 cups (452 g) shredded sharp cheddar cheese, divided

2 cups (216 g) shredded Gruyère cheese, divided

⅛ tsp cayenne pepper

½ tsp kosher salt

½ tsp black pepper

Bring a large pot of salted water to a boil over high heat. Add the pasta and cook until al dente, stirring occasionally, according to the package directions. Drain the pasta and return it to the pot. Add ¼ cup (57 g) of butter, and stir until the butter has melted and the pasta is fully coated.

Preheat the oven to 350°F (175°C).

Place a medium saucepan over medium heat and heat ⅓ cup (75 g) of butter. When the butter has melted, add the flour and cook, stirring constantly, until light brown, about 1 minute. While whisking, slowly add the milk and cream and bring to a gentle simmer. Working with a handful of cheese at a time, add 3 cups (339 g) of cheddar and 1½ cups (162 g) of Gruyère, and stir until completely melted and smooth. Add the cayenne, salt and pepper. Carefully add the cheese sauce to the pasta and stir to blend.

Grease a 9 x 13-inch (23 x 33-cm) baking dish with the remaining 2 tablespoons (28 g) of butter. Add the pasta and spread it out in an even layer. Evenly distribute the remaining 1 cup (113 g) of cheddar and ½ cup (54 g) of Gruyère on top. Bake, uncovered, until golden brown and bubbly, about 30 minutes.

Let the dish cool for 10 minutes before slicing and serving.

GNOCCHI WITH SAUSAGE & SPICY POMODORO

Ever since we discovered fresh-packed gnocchi at the grocery store, we have been absolutely hooked. These dumplings are a delicious hybrid of pasta and potato, and we don't think you sacrifice any of that light, airy, pillowy texture by going with the packaged product. In this recipe, we pair the gnocchi with tangy Italian sausage and sweet tomatoes. What makes this dish top level, though, is the presentation. After a few minutes under the broiler, the mozzarella pearls melt and the gnocchi gets crisp and golden brown. If the entire household took a vote, this recipe would easily be crowned the best dish yet.

Serves 4

1 (28-oz [794-g]) can whole peeled tomatoes

¼ cup (60 ml) extra-virgin olive oil, plus more for drizzling

2 sprigs fresh rosemary, kept whole

3 sprigs fresh basil, kept whole, plus 1 tbsp (2.5 g) chopped, for garnish, divided

2 tbsp (18 g) minced garlic

½ yellow onion, diced

2 tsp (12 g) kosher salt

1 tsp black pepper

2 tsp (2 g) dried oregano

1 tsp red pepper flakes

¼ cup (60 ml) heavy cream

1 lb (454 g) gnocchi

8 oz (226 g) ground Italian sausage

1 cup (112 g) mozzarella pearls

½ cup (50 g) fresh grated Parmesan cheese

Place the tomatoes and all of the liquid from the can in a large bowl. Using a potato masher or your hands, break the tomatoes up into smaller chunks.

Place a large, oven-safe skillet over medium heat and pour in the olive oil. When the oil is hot, add the rosemary and basil sprigs. Cook until fragrant and crispy, about 4 minutes. Remove and discard the herbs. Add the garlic and onion to the herb-flavored oil, reduce the heat to low and cook until the vegetables soften, about 5 minutes. Add the salt, pepper, oregano, red pepper flakes and crushed tomatoes and their juices and cook, uncovered, stirring occasionally, for about 35 minutes, until the sauce has thickened. Stir in the cream, cook for 3 minutes and turn off the heat.

While the sauce is cooking, bring a large pot of salted water to a boil over high heat. Add the gnocchi and cook until al dente, according to package directions.

Meanwhile, place another large skillet over medium-high heat. Cook the sausage, breaking the meat apart with a wooden spoon, until nicely browned, about 10 minutes. Transfer the meat to the sauce and stir to combine.

Preheat the broiler to high.

When the gnocchi are done, drain and arrange them in a single layer directly on top of the sauce in the skillet. Add the mozzarella pearls, sprinkle on the Parmesan cheese and drizzle with oil. Place the skillet under the broiler until the cheese is fully melted and the gnocchi is golden brown, about 8 minutes.

Garnish with the chopped basil.

ROASTED VEGGIE LASAGNA

We got the idea for this vegetable lasagna after enjoying a plate of eggplant Parmesan. We figured that if you could successfully substitute the meat for veggies in that dish without sacrificing flavor, why not do the same with lasagna? The trick to a great finished product is to roast the vegetables first until they take on some color, which adds a deep and, yes, meaty complexity to the sauce. We served this lasagna to some family members without telling them that it was meat-free, and they were none the wiser.

Serves 8

2 red bell peppers, seeded and diced

2 green bell peppers, seeded and diced

1 red onion, diced

2 medium yellow squash, diced

2 medium zucchini, diced

3 tbsp (45 ml) extra-virgin olive oil

¼ tsp crushed red pepper flakes

1½ tsp (9 g) kosher salt, divided

½ tsp black pepper

9 lasagna sheets

2 eggs

1 (15-oz [426-g]) tub whole-milk ricotta

2 cups (60 g) chopped baby spinach

3 cups (720 ml) jarred marinara (we like Rao's Homemade brand)

8 oz (226 g) shredded mozzarella

¾ cup (75 g) grated Parmesan cheese

Preheat the oven to 425°F (220°C). Grease a 9 x 13-inch (23 x 33-cm) baking dish with cooking spray.

Place the red and green bell peppers, onion, squash and zucchini on a sheet pan lined with parchment paper, drizzle with the olive oil, season with the red pepper flakes, 1 teaspoon of salt and pepper and toss to combine. Spread the vegetables evenly out on the sheet pan and bake until lightly browned, about 30 minutes.

While the veggies are roasting, bring a large pot of salted water to a boil over high heat. Add the pasta and cook until al dente, stirring occasionally, according to the package directions. Drain the pasta and arrange the noodles on another sheet pan to keep them from sticking together.

In a medium bowl, combine the eggs, ricotta and ½ teaspoon of salt and stir to blend. Set aside.

When the vegetables are done, transfer them to a large mixing bowl, add the spinach and stir until the spinach wilts, about 3 minutes. Add the marinara and stir to thoroughly coat the vegetables.

Reduce the oven to 350°F (175°C). In the greased baking dish, add one-quarter of the vegetable sauce mixture, spread it out in an even layer and arrange 3 noodles lengthwise over the top. Evenly distribute half of the ricotta and egg mixture, one-third of the mozzarella, one-third of the Parmesan and one-quarter of the remaining vegetable sauce mixture. Repeat the process with a layer of 3 noodles, the remaining ricotta and egg mixture, half of the remaining mozzarella, half of the remaining Parmesan and half of the remaining vegetable sauce mixture. Repeat the process with another layer of 3 noodles, the rest of the vegetable sauce mixture, mozzarella and Parmesan.

Spray the underside of a piece of aluminum foil before covering the baking dish and cook for 30 minutes. Remove the foil and continue cooking until golden brown and bubbly, about 15 minutes. Let the dish cool for 15 minutes before slicing and serving.

CHEESY BAKED MOSTACCIOLI

Our entire family goes crazy for lasagna, but as anybody who has ever made the dish can tell you, it's far from effortless. That's why we try to come up with stress-free alternatives like this recipe, which includes everything we love about lasagna—noodles! cheese! meat! sauce!—but does so in a more casual casserole arrangement. In this recipe, we just dollop on the ricotta cheese mixture as opposed to meticulously layering it on. And don't worry about surgically extracting the perfect slice after baking; this dish is a scooper! We made it with mostaccioli, but you could easily substitute with penne or another hollow noodle such as rigatoni. This recipe goes easy on the heat, but if you'd like to dial it up a bit, you can use spicy Italian sausage in place of the regular kind.

Serves 6

8 oz (226 g) dried mostaccioli

1½ tsp (8 ml) extra-virgin olive oil

1 medium yellow onion, diced

½ green bell pepper, diced

1 lb (454 g) ground Italian sausage

¼ tsp crushed red pepper flakes

1 tsp Italian seasoning

3 garlic cloves, minced

4½ cups (1.1 L) jarred marinara (we like Rao's Homemade brand)

Kosher salt and black pepper to taste

1 cup (246 g) ricotta or cottage cheese

1½ cups (168 g) shredded mozzarella cheese, divided

1¼ cups (125 g) grated Parmesan cheese, divided

1 egg

2 tbsp (5 g) chopped fresh basil, for garnish

Preheat the oven to 375°F (190°C). Grease an 8 x 11-inch (20 x 28-cm) baking dish with either cooking spray or olive oil.

Bring a large pot of salted water to a boil over high heat. Add the pasta and cook until al dente, stirring occasionally, according to the package directions. Drain, rinse with cold water and drain again.

Place a large skillet over medium-high heat and pour in the olive oil. When the oil is hot, add the onion, bell pepper and sausage and cook, breaking the meat apart with a wooden spoon, until nicely browned, about 8 minutes. Drain and discard the fat from the skillet before adding the red pepper flakes, Italian seasoning and garlic. Cook for 30 seconds. Reduce the heat to medium, add the marinara and simmer, stirring occasionally, for 10 minutes. Season to taste with salt and pepper.

In a small mixing bowl, combine the ricotta, ½ cup (56 g) of mozzarella, ½ cup (50 g) of Parmesan and the egg and stir to blend.

In the greased baking dish, add 1 cup (240 ml) of sauce and spread it out in an even layer. Arrange the drained pasta in an even layer on top of the sauce. Dollop the cheese and egg mixture evenly on top of the pasta. Top with the remaining sauce. Sprinkle on the remaining 1 cup (112 g) of mozzarella and ¾ cup (75 g) of Parmesan.

Bake, uncovered, until lightly golden brown and bubbly, about 25 minutes. Garnish with the basil.

BAKED ZITI WITH CHICKEN

Most baked ziti recipes call for Italian sausage, but we had some leftover rotisserie chicken, so we decided to go that route. The resulting dish is lighter, healthier and a perfect use for cooked chicken that you may be looking to use up; we don't think it sacrifices one bit of flavor or satisfaction. In fact, we now make it exclusively this way. We manage to sneak in some of those sausage-like flavors by adding Italian seasoning, which contains many of the same herbs and spices. Of course, if you prefer the classic version made with sausage, go for it! Simply cook it with the onion until the sausage is evenly browned, then mix it with the other ingredients in place of the chicken.

Serves 4

2 tbsp (36 g) plus a pinch of kosher salt

8 oz (226 g) dried ziti

1 tbsp (15 ml) extra-virgin olive oil

½ large yellow onion, chopped

2 garlic cloves, minced

2 cups (480 ml) jarred marinara (we like Rao's Homemade brand)

1 tsp dried Italian seasoning

2 tbsp (5 g) chopped fresh basil, divided

Pinch of black pepper

1½ cups (210 g) chopped cooked chicken breast

2½ cups (280 g) shredded mozzarella, divided

¾ cup (75 g) grated Parmesan cheese, divided

Preheat the oven to 350°F (175°C). Grease an 8 x 11-inch (20 x 28-cm) baking dish with either cooking spray or olive oil.

In a large pot of water, add 2 tablespoons (36 g) of salt and bring to a boil over high heat. Add the pasta and cook until al dente, stirring occasionally, according to the package directions.

Meanwhile, place a large skillet over medium heat and pour in the oil. When the oil is hot, add the onion and cook until it softens, about 5 minutes. Add the garlic and continue cooking for 1 minute. Transfer the vegetables to a large mixing bowl and add the marinara, Italian seasoning, 1 tablespoon (2.5 g) of basil and a pinch of salt and black pepper.

When the pasta is done, drain it well and add it to the bowl with the marinara. Add the chicken, 1½ cups (168 g) of mozzarella and ¼ cup (25 g) of Parmesan and mix well to combine. Pour the mixture into the greased baking dish, top with the remaining 1 cup (112 g) of mozzarella and ½ cup (50 g) of Parmesan and cook, uncovered, until the cheese is melted and golden brown, about 30 minutes. Garnish with the remaining basil.

GREEK PASTITSIO

If you're at all obsessed with Instagram like we are (and we assume that you are because you bought this cookbook!), then very likely you have seen images of the picture-perfect pastitsio. By arranging the cooked pasta piece by piece in the same direction, and carefully cutting and extracting slices, home cooks are able to snap striking images of this layered noodle dish. Don't worry if that all sounds like too much trouble because any way you stack it, this recipe is delicious. Pastitsio is often referred to as "Greek lasagna" because it's a casserole comprised of noodles, cheese and sauce, but in this case the cheese is in the form of Parmesan melted into a creamy white sauce that binds everything together. Make sure to allow the dish to cool a little before slicing for those razor-sharp edges.

Serves 10

1 lb (454 g) dried ziti

2 lbs (907 g) ground beef (90/10)

2 tbsp (30 ml) extra-virgin olive oil

1 medium white onion, diced

3 garlic cloves, minced

2 tbsp (32 g) tomato paste

1 (15-oz [426-g]) can tomato puree

½ tsp ground cinnamon

1 bay leaf

1½ tsp (9 g) kosher salt

½ tsp black pepper

CREAMY PARMESAN SAUCE

½ cup (114 g) unsalted butter

½ cup (63 g) all-purpose flour

3 cups (720 ml) whole milk

¼ tsp ground nutmeg

2 large eggs

1 cup (100 g) grated Parmesan cheese

1 tsp kosher salt

¼ tsp black pepper

Preheat the oven to 350°F (175°C). Grease a 9 x 13-inch (23 x 33-cm) baking dish with either cooking spray or olive oil.

Bring a large pot of salted water to a boil over high heat. Add the pasta and cook until al dente, stirring occasionally, according to the package directions. Drain, rinse with cold water and drain again.

Meanwhile, place a large skillet over medium-high heat. Cook the ground beef, breaking the meat apart with a wooden spoon, until nicely browned, about 7 minutes. Drain and discard the liquid from the skillet before adding the olive oil and onion. Cook until the onion begins to soften, about 7 minutes. Add the garlic, tomato paste, tomato puree, cinnamon, bay leaf, salt, pepper and ¼ cup (60 ml) of water and stir to combine. Reduce the heat to low and cook until the sauce has thickened, about 20 minutes. Remove and discard the bay leaf.

To make the creamy Parmesan sauce, in a small saucepan over medium heat, warm the butter. When the butter has melted, add the flour and cook, stirring constantly, for 2 minutes. While whisking, slowly add the milk, then whisk in the nutmeg. Reduce the heat to low and cook, stirring occasionally, for 10 minutes. Remove from the heat and allow it to cool for 10 minutes before whisking in the eggs, Parmesan, salt and pepper.

In the greased baking dish, arrange the pasta in a single direction as evenly as possible. Top with the meat sauce, spreading it out into an even layer. Pour the creamy Parmesan sauce over the meat, spreading it out into an even layer. Bake, uncovered, until golden brown, about 55 minutes.

Allow the dish to cool for 15 minutes before slicing and serving.

CHEESY CHICKEN TETRAZZINI

Once you get the hang of these baked pasta casseroles, you can really let your creativity run wild. This one is thick and creamy thanks to a roux-thickened sauce—and it's fortified with cooked chicken breast. We love adding peas for that pop of color and freshness, and a dash of nutmeg always improves béchamel-based dishes like this one. Of course, it all gets baked beneath a blanket of cheese until golden brown and bubbly!

Serves 6–8

2 tbsp (30 ml) extra-virgin olive oil

8 oz (226 g) white mushrooms, thinly sliced

1 medium yellow onion, diced

½ tbsp (2 g) dried thyme

4 garlic cloves, minced

½ cup (120 ml) dry white wine

1 lb (454 g) cubed cooked skinless chicken breast

10 oz (283 g) dried linguine

3 tbsp (42 g) butter

⅓ cup (41 g) all-purpose flour

4 cups (960 ml) whole milk

1 cup (240 ml) heavy cream

1 cup (240 ml) chicken broth

1 tsp kosher salt

½ tsp black pepper

⅛ tsp ground nutmeg

½ cup (73 g) frozen peas

¼ cup (15 g) chopped fresh flat-leaf parsley

1 cup (112 g) shredded mozzarella cheese

¾ cup (85 g) shredded cheddar cheese

½ cup (50 g) grated Parmesan cheese

Place a large skillet over medium-high heat and pour in the oil. When the oil is hot, add the mushrooms and cook until softened, about 4 minutes. Add the onion and thyme and cook, stirring occasionally, until the onion is translucent, about 5 minutes. Add the garlic and cook, stirring occasionally, until fragrant, about 1 minute. Add the wine and cook for 4 minutes. Transfer this mixture to a bowl, add the cooked chicken and set aside.

Preheat the oven to 350°F (175°C).

Bring a large pot of salted water to a boil over high heat. Add the pasta and cook until al dente, stirring occasionally, according to the package directions. Drain and set aside.

Meanwhile, place the skillet over medium heat and warm the butter. When the butter has melted, add the flour and cook, stirring constantly, for 2 minutes. While whisking, slowly add the milk, cream and chicken broth. Add the salt, pepper and nutmeg and whisk until smooth. Bring to a simmer and cook, while whisking, until the sauce thickens slightly, about 6 minutes. Add the cooked pasta and the chicken-mushroom mixture and stir until the pasta is completely coated in sauce. Add the peas and parsley and stir to blend.

Grease a 9 x 13-inch (23 x 33-cm) baking dish with cooking spray or butter. Transfer the pasta mixture to the baking dish, top evenly with the mozzarella, cheddar and Parmesan, cover with aluminum foil and cook for 30 minutes. Remove the foil and continue cooking until lightly golden brown and bubbly, about 15 minutes.

Allow the dish to cool for 10 minutes before slicing and serving.

FLAVOR— PACKED SOUPS & PASTA SALADS

When it comes to the pasta salad recipes in this chapter, we really let our creativity run wild. Unlike the more famous or classic recipes elsewhere in the book, where we strive to remain faithful to the originals, salads gave us an opportunity to have some fun. I mean, how great does a pasta salad version of the beloved BLT sandwich sound (page 127)? (Spoiler alert: super-great!) For something lighter, brighter and more wholesome, check out the Veggie Greek Pasta Salad (page 133), which is loaded with fresh, crisp veggies.

Most of these salads work equally well for lunch or a light dinner, making them really flexible. They also hold up well for days in the fridge—ideal for meal-prep situations.

Even though we live in L.A., there are plenty of times when we crave a big bowl of comforting soup. And in our very humble opinion, the best way to step up your soup game is by adding noodles! Fat, toothsome egg noodles enrich a pot of Creamy Chicken Noodle Soup (page 129), plump gnocchi transform Zuppa Toscana (page 119) with sausage and kale into a heavenly meal, and if you've never enjoyed a creamy tomato soup loaded with three-cheese tortellini (page 130), just wait until you dip your spoon into the version we have here.

STRAWBERRY–BALSAMIC PASTA SALAD

This recipe elevates one of our favorite summer salads into a refreshing and interesting pasta salad that would be great as a light lunch or dinner starter. The sweet/salty flavor combination of strawberries and feta cheese is really something special. If you like blue cheese, feel free to use that instead of feta. We add crunchy candied nuts for texture and a simple but captivating dressing to tie it all together.

Serves 4

2 tbsp (30 ml) balsamic vinegar glaze

2 tbsp (30 ml) extra-virgin olive oil

8 oz (226 g) dried farfalle

1 cup (20 g) arugula

1 cup (166 g) sliced strawberries

½ cup (75 g) crumbled feta

½ cup (80 g) sliced red onion

½ cup (55 g) chopped glazed or candied pecans

In a small bowl, whisk to combine the balsamic vinegar glaze and olive oil.

Bring a large pot of salted water to a boil over high heat. Add the pasta and cook until al dente, stirring occasionally, according to the package directions. Drain, rinse with cold water and drain again.

In a large bowl, combine the arugula, strawberries, feta, onion, pecans and pasta. Add the balsamic vinegar glaze mixture and toss to combine.

ZUPPA TOSCANA

If you're in search of the ultimate cold-weather warmer, look no further than this recipe. We confess that we first fell in love with Zuppa Toscana during a visit to Olive Garden; what's not to love about a creamy chicken soup with potatoes, sausage and kale? After tinkering with various homemade versions of the recipe, we landed on this one as the standout, thanks to the addition of gnocchi in place of the customary potatoes. All we can say is "wow!" As is our formula throughout this book, we combine from-scratch techniques with time-saving ingredients to land delicious, doable results. In this recipe, we go with a good-quality boxed chicken stock and think it's the perfect compromise between effort and outcome.

Serves 6

1 lb (454 g) ground hot Italian sausage

8 slices of bacon, diced

1 medium yellow onion, diced

2 garlic cloves, minced

4 cups (960 ml) chicken broth

½ tsp kosher salt

¼ tsp black pepper

½ bunch kale, stemmed and roughly chopped

1 lb (454 g) gnocchi

1 cup (240 ml) heavy cream

In a large saucepan over medium heat, cook the sausage, breaking the meat apart with a wooden spoon, until nicely browned, about 10 minutes. Transfer the meat to a paper towel–lined plate to drain. Drain and discard all but 1 tablespoon (15 ml) of the fat from the skillet. Cook the bacon until crispy, about 8 minutes. Transfer the bacon to a paper towel–lined plate to drain. Drain and discard all but 1 tablespoon (15 ml) of the fat from the skillet.

In the same saucepan, cook the onion until it begins to soften, about 5 minutes. Add the garlic and cook for 30 seconds. Raise the heat to medium-high and add the chicken broth, salt, pepper and cooked sausage. When the soup reaches a simmer, add the kale and gnocchi and cook until the gnocchi begin to float, about 5 minutes. Stir in the cream.

Remove from the heat, divide among bowls and garnish with the bacon.

CAPRESE PASTA SALAD

One of our favorite seasonal dishes is the classic Italian Caprese salad. This recipe turns that light summer salad into a more satisfying main dish thanks to the addition of pasta. We think rotini is the perfect pasta shape because it grabs and holds the tangy vinaigrette, but you can substitute whatever bite-size variety you have on hand. Another tweak that we believe improves on the conventional arrangement is the utilization of mozzarella balls in place of sliced or quartered cheese. The final drizzle of sticky-sweet balsamic glaze takes it to the next level and really ties everything together. This salad gets even better as it sits in the fridge for a couple of days.

Serves 4

⅓ cup (80 ml) extra-virgin olive oil

1 tbsp (15 ml) balsamic vinegar

⅓ tsp dried oregano

3 tbsp (8 g) chopped fresh basil

2 tbsp (36 g) plus a pinch of kosher salt, divided

Pinch of black pepper

3 cups (447 g) cherry tomatoes, halved

8 oz (226 g) mozzarella balls

8 oz (226 g) dried rotini or pasta of your choice

2 tbsp (30 ml) balsamic glaze, for garnish

In a large mixing bowl, whisk to combine the olive oil, balsamic vinegar, oregano, basil, pinch of salt and pinch of pepper. Add the tomatoes and mozzarella and toss to combine. Set aside for at least 25 minutes to let the flavors meld.

Meanwhile, add 2 tablespoons (36 g) of salt to a large pot of water and bring to a boil over high heat. Add the pasta and cook until al dente, stirring occasionally, according to the package directions. Drain, rinse with cold water until cooled, then drain again very well. Add the pasta to the tomato and mozzarella salad and toss to combine. Taste and adjust the seasoning, adding additional salt and pepper if desired.

Divide the pasta salad among four bowls and drizzle with the balsamic glaze.

NIKU UDON SOUP

We first tasted this noodle soup on a trip to San Francisco a few years back. Maybe it was the cold and rainy weather at the time, but we both thought that it was the most comforting and delicious food in the entire world. In Japanese cooking, the secret to amazing broths and soups often starts with hondashi, which provides a wonderful flavor base. To that base we add chewy udon, savory beef and mushrooms and mild-flavored but wonderfully textured fish cakes. The next time the thermometer dips and the umbrellas come out, give this recipe a try.

Serves 4

1 (8-g) packet hondashi soup stock base

4 tbsp (60 ml) soy sauce, divided

2 tbsp (30 ml) mirin

2 tsp (8 g) sugar

½ tsp kosher salt

2 tbsp (30 ml) vegetable oil

12 oz (340 g) beef, thinly sliced (top sirloin or ribeye)

8 oz (226 g) fresh udon

1½ cups (45 g) fresh spinach

2½ oz (70 g) shitake mushrooms, thinly sliced

2 oz (57 g) fish cakes, sliced

2 scallions, thinly sliced, for garnish

In a medium saucepan, bring 5 cups (1.2 L) of water to a boil over high heat. Add the hondashi, 2 tablespoons (30 ml) of soy sauce, mirin, sugar and salt and stir to combine. Cover and reduce the heat to low to keep the broth warm while preparing the other elements.

Place a large skillet over medium-high heat and pour in the vegetable oil. When the oil is hot, add the beef in a single layer and cook, without stirring, until lightly browned, about 2 minutes. Flip the beef, add the remaining soy sauce and cook, while stirring, until the sauce thickens slightly, about 1 minute. Remove it from the heat.

Bring a large pot of water to a boil over high heat. Add the noodles and cook, stirring occasionally, according to the package directions. Without draining the pot, transfer the noodles directly into four serving bowls. To the boiling water, add the spinach and mushrooms and cook for 1 minute. Drain the vegetables and divide evenly among the four bowls.

Ladle the soup broth into the bowls, top with the cooked beef, fish cakes and scallions.

RAINBOW ITALIAN PASTA SALAD

We love shopping at our neighborhood gourmet markets, where they have coolers filled with amazing ready-to-eat foods. One of our favorite finds is this bright, fresh and colorful pasta salad. Unfortunately, it's too expensive to eat as often as we would like, so we decided to come up with our own version. We whip up a big batch of this salad and pop it in the fridge, so we always have some on hand for a quick, healthy side dish or portable lunch. It is equally delicious cold or at room temperature, and the flavor improves after a couple of days as the flavors marry. We think tri-color pasta adds a nice visual boost, but regular rotini or fusilli tastes the same. Trust us, you cannot mess this dish up.

Serves 4

PASTA SALAD

2 tbsp (36 g) kosher salt

8 oz (226 g) tri-color rotini

½ cup (75 g) halved cherry tomatoes

¼ cup (12 g) sliced scallions

¼ cup (23 g) sliced pepperoncini

½ cup (90 g) halved Kalamata olives

½ cup (75 g) chopped bell pepper

⅛ cup (5 g) chopped fresh basil

½ cup (112 g) mozzarella pearls or balls

½ cup (70 g) chopped Genoa salami or ham or pepperoni

DRESSING

¼ cup (60 ml) extra-virgin olive oil

¼ cup (60 ml) red wine vinegar

¼ tsp kosher salt

¼ tsp black pepper

¼ tsp dried oregano

To make the pasta salad, to a large pot of water, add the salt and bring to a boil over high heat. Add the pasta and cook until al dente, stirring occasionally, according to the package directions. Drain, rinse with cold water until cooled, then drain again.

Meanwhile, to make the dressing, in a large mixing bowl, whisk to combine the olive oil, red wine vinegar, salt, pepper and oregano.

Add the cooked pasta to the bowl with the dressing and toss to combine. Add the tomatoes, scallions, pepperoncini, olives, bell pepper, basil, mozzarella and salami and toss to combine.

Serve the dish immediately, or place it in the refrigerator to enjoy later for up to 5 days.

BLT FUSILLI

If you love BLT sandwiches, then you're going to love this recipe, which transforms that summer staple into a refreshing and flavorful pasta salad. While it might be a bit of a stretch to call this salad "healthy"—*it has a lot of bacon!*—it is quick and easy and equally great as a starter, side dish or main course. We use Italian dressing in this recipe because we think the flavors marry well together, but go ahead and use Caesar or something creamy like ranch if you prefer. This salad would also be great with crispy chopped romaine in place of the leaf lettuce.

Serves 4

8 oz (226 g) dried fusilli

16 strips bacon, diced

6 cups (330 g) chopped green leaf lettuce

2 cups (330 g) halved grape tomatoes

1 cup (160 g) chopped red onion

⅔ cup (160 ml) Italian dressing

Freshly ground black pepper to taste

Bring a large pot of salted water to a boil over high heat. Add the pasta and cook until al dente, stirring occasionally, according to the package directions. Drain, rinse with cold water until cooled, then drain again.

Meanwhile, place a large skillet over medium-high heat. Cook the bacon, stirring occasionally, until crisp, about 5 minutes. Transfer to a paper towel–lined plate to drain.

In a large mixing bowl, place the lettuce, tomatoes, onion, pasta, bacon and Italian dressing and toss to combine.

Plate and season with pepper, as desired.

CREAMY CHICKEN NOODLE SOUP

The only thing more enjoyable on a cold winter day than a steaming bowl of chicken noodle soup is a big bowl of this ultra-cozy and creamy version. This recipe has it all: aromatic vegetables, tender noodles, plenty of chicken and a rich broth made all the better thanks to the addition of a silky béchamel. We start with store-bought chicken broth, but by cooking the chicken, herbs and vegetables in it, we really enhance its flavor. A pinch of red pepper flakes brings a hint of heat that adds complexity to the flavors, but feel free to omit it if you prefer.

Serves 4

8 oz (226 g) wide egg noodles

1½ tbsp (22 ml) extra-virgin olive oil

3 celery ribs, diced

3 carrots, diced

1 medium yellow onion, diced

3 garlic cloves, minced

3 (6- to 8-oz [170- to 226-g]) boneless, skinless chicken breasts, cubed

4 cups (960 ml) low-sodium chicken broth

2 bay leaves

3 tbsp (12 g) chopped fresh parsley

⅛ tsp crushed red pepper flakes

Kosher salt and black pepper

4 tbsp (56 g) butter

4 tbsp (32 g) all-purpose flour

2½ cups (600 ml) 2-percent or whole milk

½ cup (120 ml) heavy cream

Bring a large pot of salted water to a boil over high heat. Add the pasta and cook until al dente, stirring occasionally, according to the package directions. Drain, rinse with cold water and drain again.

Meanwhile, place a large saucepan over medium heat and pour in the olive oil. Add the celery, carrots and onion and cook, stirring occasionally, until the vegetables soften, about 4 minutes. Add the garlic and cook until fragrant, about 1 minute. Add the chicken, chicken broth, bay leaves, parsley, red pepper flakes and a few pinches of salt and pepper and bring to a boil. Reduce the heat to low, cover and simmer gently until the chicken registers 165°F (75°C) on an instant-read thermometer, about 15 minutes. Remove and discard the bay leaves.

Meanwhile, place a medium saucepan over medium heat and warm the butter. When the butter has melted, add the flour and cook, stirring constantly, for 2 minutes. While whisking, slowly add the milk, then, continuing to whisk, slowly add the cream. Bring to a boil, whisking throughout. Carefully transfer this mixture to the chicken soup. Add the drained noodles and stir to blend.

TOMATO TORTELLINI SOUP

One of the simplest and most economical ways to transform a soup into a hearty meal, we have found, is by adding prepared tortellini. We look for the fresh, refrigerated packages because they cook up right in the broth in no time at all. Our favorite is filled with a three-cheese blend of ricotta, Romano and Parmesan. In addition to the tender, cheesy dumplings, this soup gets an added boost from zesty Italian sausage and rich cream. Just before serving, finish it off with a sprinkle of freshly grated cheese and chopped fresh basil.

Serves 4

8 oz (226 g) ground Italian sausage

1½ tbsp (22 ml) extra-virgin olive oil

1 medium yellow onion, chopped

⅛ tsp black pepper

3 garlic cloves, minced

1 tsp dried oregano

½ tsp dried thyme

1 small zucchini, diced

1½ cups (360 ml) chicken broth

1 (28-oz [794-g]) can crushed tomatoes

9 oz (255 g) refrigerated packaged cheese tortellini

¼ cup (60 ml) heavy cream

Grated Parmesan cheese, for garnish

Chopped fresh basil, for garnish

Place a large skillet over medium-high heat. Cook the sausage, breaking the meat apart with a wooden spoon, until lightly browned, about 8 minutes. Remove from the heat, drain any accumulated fat and set the sausage aside on a paper towel-lined plate.

Place a large saucepan over medium-high heat and pour in the olive oil. Add the onion and black pepper and cook, stirring occasionally, until the onion softens, about 4 minutes. Add the garlic, oregano, thyme and zucchini and cook, stirring occasionally, until the vegetables soften, about 2 minutes.

Add the chicken broth, tomatoes and tortellini, cover and bring to a simmer. Reduce the heat to low and cook until the tortellini are done, about 8 minutes depending on the brand you're using (follow the time listed on the package instructions). Once the tortellini are done, add the cooked sausage to the soup pot and stir to blend. Add the cream, stir and cook for 1 minute.

Divide the soup among four bowls and top with the Parmesan and basil, to taste.

VEGGIE GREEK PASTA SALAD

As you've probably noticed in this chapter, we go out of our way to create healthy, simple and flavorful pasta salad recipes, like our Rainbow Italian Pasta Salad (page 124) and Caprese Pasta Salad (page 120). Similar to those winning dishes, this one is crisp, crunchy and nutritious. There are loads of fresh vegetables, which get tossed with fun-shaped shells in a honey-kissed vinaigrette. The addition of Kalamata olives and feta cheese give this salad a Mediterranean flair. Like all of the pasta salads in this book, this one works great as a salad, side dish or main course and just gets better with time.

Serves 4

8 oz (226 g) medium pasta shells

½ cup (120 ml) extra-virgin olive oil

⅓ cup (80 ml) red wine vinegar

Juice of a small lemon

2 tsp (10 ml) Dijon mustard

2 tsp (10 ml) honey

½ tsp dried oregano

¼ tsp kosher salt

¼ tsp black pepper

½ cup (80 g) chopped red onion

½ cup (90 g) Kalamata olives, pitted and halved

½ cup (100 g) chopped artichoke hearts, drained

½ cup (75 g) diced orange bell pepper

½ cup (75 g) diced red bell pepper

1 cup (149 g) cherry tomatoes, halved

½ cup (75 g) crumbled feta cheese

Bring a large pot of salted water to a boil over high heat. Add the pasta and cook until al dente, stirring occasionally, according to the package directions. Drain, rinse with cold water and drain again.

In a large mixing bowl, whisk to combine the olive oil, red wine vinegar, lemon juice, mustard, honey, oregano, salt and pepper. Add the red onion, olives and artichoke hearts and toss. Add the bell peppers, tomatoes and drained pasta and toss to combine.

Gently stir in most of the feta, saving a tablespoon (9 g) or so to sprinkle on the top. Serve immediately or chill in the fridge until ready to serve. It will keep for up to a week.

SPICY FISH BALL SOUP

This recipe is for all you spice hounds out there because IT IS HOT! Please proceed with caution and do not serve this dish to children because it is a true Sichuan-style hot and spicy soup. If you've ever enjoyed hot pot in an Asian restaurant, this is likely the type of tongue-tingling broth that was used. We use a high-quality Sichuan soup base to keep things simple and to allow for more creativity with the add-ins. The sky is truly the limit in terms of what kinds of vegetables, meats, seafood and noodles you can add to the soup. This one features fish balls, which have a unique fluffy, springy texture that people tend to love or not. Obviously, we love it! Fish cakes are also made from ground fish and are fully cooked, but have a different taste and texture. You can find both in the freezer section of Asian markets.

Serves 4–6

1 (7-oz [198-g]) pouch Sichuan soup base (we like Lee Kum Kee)

15 oz (425 g) fish balls (thawed if frozen)

Kosher salt and/or soy sauce to taste (optional)

1 lb (454 g) flat rice noodles or pho noodles

3 oz (85 g) fish cake (thawed if frozen), sliced

4 oz (113 g) beansprouts

4 scallions, thinly sliced, for garnish

2 tbsp (18 g) fried garlic, for garnish

In a large saucepan, combine the soup mix with 10 cups (2.4 L) of cold water and bring to a boil over high heat. Add the fish balls, reduce the heat to low and simmer for 20 minutes. Taste and adjust the seasoning, adding salt and/or soy sauce (if desired).

Meanwhile, bring a large pot of water to a boil and prepare the noodles according to the package instructions. Drain them and divide among serving bowls. Divide the fish cake slices and beansprouts evenly among the bowls.

When the soup is done, divide the fish balls and broth evenly among the bowls. Top with the scallions and fried garlic.

SURF 'N' TURF WONTON NOODLE SOUP

We know what you're thinking: "*This recipe looks complicated, Larone and Tiffani!*" While this double-noodle soup might require more steps than usual, we promise that none of them are difficult—and the results are totally worth the effort. Throughout this book we utilize shortcuts like jarred marinara and boxed broth to eliminate some big hurdles so you can spend more time with the ones you love. But trust us, these shrimp and pork wontons are a million times better made fresh compared to the ones sold frozen in markets. Plus, we think that the filling and folding process makes for an enjoyable family activity! When it comes to garnishes, the sky's the limit, but we love adding fresh scallions, sliced shitakes, cubed tofu and some chili crisp to finish this dish off right.

Serves 4

BROTH

8 cups (2 L) chicken broth

1 garlic clove, lightly smashed

3 tsp (45 ml) sesame oil

1 tsp soy sauce

2 scallions, halved

Kosher salt and black pepper to taste

SHRIMP WONTONS

8 medium shrimp, peeled and deveined

½ scallion, thinly sliced

½ garlic clove, minced

½ tsp Shaoxing wine

¼ tsp sesame oil

½ tsp soy sauce

⅛ tsp black pepper

14 wonton wrappers (thawed if frozen)

PORK WONTONS

4 oz (113 g) ground pork

½ scallion, thinly sliced

½ garlic clove, minced

½ tsp Shaoxing wine

¼ tsp sesame oil

½ tsp soy sauce

⅛ tsp black pepper

14 wonton wrappers (thawed if frozen)

SOUP

1 bunch baby bok choy

8 oz (226 g) fresh wonton noodles

3 scallions, thinly sliced, for garnish

2 oz (57 g) shitake mushrooms, thinly sliced, for garnish

3 oz (85 g) cubed tofu, for garnish (optional)

Chili crisp or chili oil, for garnish (optional)

(continued)

To make the broth, in a large pot, combine 4 cups (960 ml) of water, the chicken broth, garlic, sesame oil, soy sauce and scallions. Bring to a simmer over medium heat and cook, uncovered, for 30 minutes. Taste and adjust the seasoning, adding salt and pepper if desired. Remove and discard the scallions and garlic clove. Cover and keep warm over low heat.

To make the shrimp wontons, while the broth is cooking, place the shrimp in a food processor. Pulse until it's an almost smooth paste, about 5 times, making sure to occasionally scrape down the sides. Transfer the paste to a medium mixing bowl and add the scallion, garlic, wine, sesame oil, soy sauce and black pepper and mix well to combine.

Working with one wonton wrapper at a time, lightly moisten the edges of the wrapper with water, place 1 teaspoon of the shrimp filling in the center, fold the wrapper in half on the diagonal and gently squeeze to seal. Repeat with the remaining 13 wrappers. Refrigerate until needed.

To make the pork wontons, in a medium mixing bowl, combine the pork, scallion, garlic, wine, sesame oil, soy sauce and black pepper and mix well.

Working with one wonton wrapper at a time, lightly moisten the edges of the wrapper with water, place 1 teaspoon of the pork filling in the center, fold the wrapper in half on the diagonal and gently squeeze to seal. Repeat with the remaining 13 wrappers. Refrigerate until needed.

To build the soup, bring a large pot of water to a boil over high heat. Add the bok choy and cook for 1 minute. Transfer the bok choy to a strainer with a slotted spoon, rinse with cold water until cool and drain. Evenly divide the bok choy among four bowls.

Add the wonton noodles to the boiling water and cook for 1 minute. Remove, rinse with cold water and drain. Evenly divide the noodles among the four bowls.

Add the shrimp and pork wontons to the boiling water and cook until they float, about 5 minutes. Evenly divide the wontons among the four bowls. Fill the bowls with hot broth and garnish with the scallions, mushrooms, tofu (if using) and chili crisp (if using), as desired.

ACKNOWLEDGMENTS

We would like to thank Page Street for presenting us with the opportunity to release our first cookbook to the world. This book took a lot of hard work and late hours, but it was all worth it in the end, thanks to them. Thank you to Sarah Monroe for managing the project and checking in with words of encouragement and guidance. Thank you to Douglas Trattner for the countless calls, assistance and advice. You truly have a way with words and your experience in the cookbook industry has been vital to this project.

Thank you to Leonette "Nene" Thompson for encouragement, recipe assistance and taste testing. We are truly honored to have cooked all of these recipes for you. Thank you to Ira, Riley and Marsel Thompson for being the best taste testers and providing constructive criticism.

A special thank you to all of our Instagram followers that show us so much love on a daily basis, and especially those that ask us for recipes. We hope you all enjoy this book as much as we did cooking for it.

ABOUT THE AUTHORS

Larone Thompson is a content creator, photographer and home chef, born and raised in Los Angeles, California. Tiffani Thompson is a content creator, graphic designer and photographer. She was born in Southern California. Together, Larone and Tiffani are the co-creators and curators for the @noodleworship social media account and brand, as well as @surfnoturf and @tastethisnext.

Larone & Tiffani Thompson have been married for 7 years and have two children, Riley and Marsel, with Jada on the way. Their photos and videos have been shared all over social media by Complex, *ABC7 News*, BuzzFeed and numerous high-profile musicians. This is their first published book. Learn more at www.tastethisnext.com.

Outside the cooking world, Larone is also an entrepreneur, mentor, investor, hip hop enthusiast, video gamer and household comedian. You can connect with him on Instagram at @nintendough84. Tiffani is also an entrepreneur and music enthusiast. You can follow her personal life at @soseductiff.

INDEX